EGO, ATTACHMENT AND LIBERATION

LAMA YESHE

Ego, Attachment and Liberation

OVERCOMING YOUR MENTAL BUREAUCRACY
A FIVE-DAY MEDITATION COURSE

Edited by Nicholas Ribush

LAMA YESHE WISDOM ARCHIVE • BOSTON
www.LamaYeshe.com

A non-profit charitable organization for the benefit of all
sentient beings and an affiliate of the Foundation for
the Preservation of the Mahayana Tradition
www.fpmt.org

First published 2006
20,000 copies for free distribution

LAMA YESHE WISDOM ARCHIVE
PO BOX 356, WESTON, MA 02493, USA

ISBN 1-891868-18-7

10 9 8 7 6 5 4 3 2 1

Cover photograph by Carol Royce-Wilder
Cover line art by Robert Beer
Designed by Gopa & Ted2, Inc.

Following the excellent example of Wisdom Publications,
we have decided to produce this book with environmental
mindfulness and print it on 50% PCW recycled paper. As a result we
have saved the following resources: 54 trees, 2,506 lbs. of solid waste,
19,517 gallons of water, 4,702 lbs. of greenhouse gases and 37 million
BTUs of energy. For more information, please visit our Web site.

Please contact the LAMA YESHE WISDOM ARCHIVE
for more copies of this and our other free books

··· Contents ···

Vajrapani Institute, 1983

···Publisher's Acknowledgments···

WE ARE EXTREMELY GRATEFUL to our friends and supporters who have made it possible for the LAMA YESHE WISDOM ARCHIVE to both exist and function: to Lama Yeshe and Lama Zopa Rinpoche, whose kindness is impossible to repay; to Peter and Nicole Kedge and Venerable Ailsa Cameron for their initial work on the ARCHIVE; to Venerable Roger Kunsang, Lama Zopa's tireless assistant, for his kindness and consideration; and to our sustaining supporters: Barry & Connie Hershey, Joan Halsall, Roger & Claire Ash-Wheeler, Claire Atkins, Thubten Yeshe, Richard Gere, Doren & Mary Harper, Tom & Suzanne Castles, Lily Chang Wu and Hawk Furman.

We are also deeply grateful to all those who have become members of the ARCHIVE over the past few years. Details of our membership program may be found at the back of this book, and if you are not a member, please do consider joining up. Due to the kindness of those who have, we now have several editors working on our vast collection of teachings for the benefit of all. We have posted our list of individual and corporate members on our Web site, www.LamaYeshe.com. We also thank Henry & Catherine Lau and S. S. Lim for their help with our membership program in Singapore and Serina Yap for her help with our membership program in Malaysia. Thank you all so much for your foresight and kindness.

In particular, we thank Janet Hintermann for her major contribution to this book, made in gratitude for the kindness and generosity of her parents, Jean and Evelyn, and dedicated to their and all other sentient beings' happiness, well being and enlightenment.

We also thank our other members—Chandrakirti Centre (Phillipa Rutherford & Bruce Farley), Tim Burress, Betsy U. Chang, Elli and Lindsay Pratt, Chin-Yu Lai, Lee Tin Yan, Adrian Dec, Lynne Sonenberg, Christine Arlington, Sandra and Will Moss-Manson, Len Martin Jr., Lam Lai Peng, Richard Navitsky, Yvonne Zwart, Wai-Ming William Chan, Brian Ko-Ming Li, Siew Yong Gnanalingam, Chia Chu Hong & Soon Chun, Chan Ai Hup, Philip Suping Lo, Judith Kondo, Vajrapani Institute, Laura Linscomb, Linda McConnell, Stefanie Harvey and several anonymous donors—who also responded to our request for contributions to this book.

In addition, I would like to express my appreciation for the kindness and compassion of all those other generous benefactors who have contributed funds to our work since we began publishing free books. Thankfully, you are too numerous to mention individually in this book, but we value highly each and every donation made to spreading the Dharma for the sake of the kind mother sentient beings and now pay tribute to you all on our Web site. Thank you so much.

Finally, I would like to thank the many kind people who have asked that their donations be kept anonymous; the volunteers who have given so generously of their time to help us with our mailings, especially Therese Miller; my wife, Wendy Cook, for her constant help and support; our dedicated office staff, Jennifer Barlow and Sonal Shastri; Ven.

Thubten Labdron (Trisha Donnelly) for her help with archiving and editing; Ven. Bob Alcorn for his incredible work on our Lama Yeshe DVDs; Robert Curtis for kindly hosting our audio and other files on his server; Veronica Kaczmarowski, Evelyn Williames, FPMT Australia & Mandala Books (Brisbane) for much appreciated assistance with our distribution in Australia; Dennis Heslop, Philip Bradley and our other friends at Wisdom Books (London) for their great help with our distribution in Europe; our volunteer transcribers; and Greg Sneddon, Dr. Su Hung and Anne Pottage in Australia for their help with our audio work.

If you, dear reader, would like to join this noble group of open-hearted altruists by contributing to the production of more free books by Lama Yeshe or Lama Zopa Rinpoche or to any other aspect of the LAMA YESHE WISDOM ARCHIVE's work, please contact us to find out how.

—Dr. Nicholas Ribush

Through the merit of having contributed to the spread of the Buddha's teachings for the sake of all sentient beings, may our benefactors and their families and friends have long and healthy lives, all happiness, and may all their Dharma wishes be instantly fulfilled.

· · · · ·

Lama Yeshe and the editor at Lake Arrowhead, California, July 1975

··· Editor's Introduction ···

O UR PREVIOUS FREE Lama Yeshe books, *Becoming Your Own Therapist, Make Your Mind an Ocean* and *The Peaceful Stillness of the Silent Mind*, contain public talks Lama gave in Australia and New Zealand in 1975 on his and Lama Zopa Rinpoche's second world tour. I was fortunate enough to be their roadie and teaching assistant on that wonderful voyage and more than thirty years later, the memory still resonates strongly in my mind.

As well as giving his many public talks, Lama also led a five-day meditation course for about one hundred students at Dromana, near Melbourne.[1] This book contains his teachings and meditations from that event and, as its title suggests, Lama's focus was on the shortcomings of ego and attachment—the main causes of all our suffering and problems—and how to overcome them.

As the lamas always tell us, the way to use Dharma teachings is as a mirror for the mind, and during this course—especially during the first couple of days' teachings, which were not specifically labeled meditation sessions—he would pause to give us time to reflect on what he had just said; to contemplate its meaning and see if we could recognize ourselves in it. These breaks are indicated in the hope that you, dear reader,

---

[1] At the Don Bosco Camp, Safety Beach, Dromana, March 28 through April 1. (www.donboscocamp.org)

will also pause for a moment to think about what Lama has just told you. For that's another way to listen to teachings—to take them as personal advice and to apply to yourself what you've just heard or read.

In his opening address, Lama indicates his intention by saying, "If over the next five days you can begin to recognize the reality of your own nature, this meditation course will have been worthwhile. Therefore, dedicate your actions during this time to discovering inner freedom through recognizing the negative characteristics of your own uncontrolled mind."

This is also our hope in publishing this book and bringing it to you.

I thank Jennifer Barlow and Wendy Cook for their kind editorial suggestions.

··· 1 ···

Making Space for Wisdom

Prostrations

[Lama Yeshe makes three prostrations.]

WHY DO WE MAKE prostrations at the beginning of teaching and meditation sessions? It's to beat our ego down a bit. Egocentric pride looks at things very superficially and never sees the nature of reality.

When we prostrate, we're not prostrating to the material objects on the altar but paying homage to true, understanding wisdom. People who have taken Dharma teachings before know this well; I mention it mainly for new students.

Prostration isn't just a Buddhist custom. To make sure that giving teachings does not become an ego-trip, even great teachers like His Holiness the Dalai Lama will prostrate before they get up on the throne. In fact, to diminish pride and become more grounded in reality, both teacher and student should prostrate before a teaching. Otherwise, there's no space for understanding wisdom. The proud mind is like a desert; nothing can grow in a mind full of pride. That's why we prostrate toward the altar prior to giving and taking teachings.

In our everyday lives we prostrate to things that are not worthwhile.

Of course, we don't say that we're prostrating, but in fact we constantly pay homage to our pride and ego. Instead of prostrating to pride and ego we should prostrate to understanding wisdom.

The Tibetan term for prostration is *chag-tsäl*. In Sanskrit, *chag* is *mudra*. The interpretive meaning of mudra is wisdom; understanding knowledge-wisdom is the actual mudra. *Tsäl* means to bow down before or pay homage or obeisance to something. Therefore, *chag-tsäl* means to bow down to wisdom, and when we prostrate our mental attitude should be one that recognizes the harmful nature of egocentric pride and understands that knowledge-wisdom is the only worthwhile guide.

If you don't have this respectful attitude you might as well not bow down. If you're not prostrating with your mind there's no need to prostrate physically simply for the sake of show or custom. Tradition is not that important. But if you recognize how your pride functions and prostrate to wisdom instead, that is very effective, and doing so makes prostrating a means of training your mind.

This five-day course

Whether or not this five-day meditation course becomes beneficial is up to you; it depends on your own mind. It's not a lama thing; I'm not going to bring you to enlightenment in this short time. Instead of having too many expectations of the lama, it's better that you generate a pure motivation for being here. Expectations cause mental problems; instead of being positive, they become negative. Instead of expecting something, dedicate in the following way:

"Over the next five days, I am going to investigate and try to discover

and understand my own nature and recognize my own false conceptions and mistaken actions. From the time of my birth up till now, I have
been under the control of my conditioned, dissatisfied mind. Even
though my only desire is for lasting happiness and enjoyment, I am constantly tossed up and down by external conditions. I am completely
oppressed by my uncontrolled, dissatisfied mind. I have no freedom
whatsoever, even though my fickle, arrogant mind always pretends,
'I'm happy; I'm free.' Any happiness I do experience is fleeting. If
another person were to persecute or oppress me, I couldn't stand it for
even a day, but if I check more deeply I will see that from the moment
of my birth, my uncontrolled mind has not given me the slightest
chance to be freely joyful. It has been completely enslaved by external
conditions."

If over the next five days you can begin to recognize the reality of
your own nature, this meditation course will have been worthwhile.
Therefore, dedicate your actions during this time to discovering inner
freedom through recognizing the negative characteristics of your own
uncontrolled mind.

Think, "I completely dedicate the next five days of my life to discovering inner peace—not only for myself but for all living beings throughout the universe. From the moment of my birth, I have been utterly
under the control of the totally unrealistic and ridiculous philosophy of
attachment and always put myself first, wanting victory for myself and
defeat for others. Therefore, the most meaningful thing I can do is to

completely donate the next five days of my life to others, with no expectation of receiving anything myself."

Pure motivation is a function of the wise and open mind, which is the total opposite of the narrow, psychologically defiled, obsessed mind that is overly concerned for one's own benefit and welfare. Completely donating your life to others has a great effect on your internal world. But this is not an emotional gesture—dedicating yourself to others doesn't mean stripping naked and giving them all your clothes. Dedicating yourself to others is an act of wisdom, not emotion, and derives from discovering how harmful the mind of attachment is; how for countless lives attachment has accumulated in your mind, occupying and polluting it completely.

Thus, the purpose of this meditation course is not simply for receiving information. It's a school for training your mind. If during this course you can learn how to act out of wisdom instead of ignorance, out of universal consciousness instead of narrow conceptions, it will have been extremely worthwhile.

If your mind is possessed by expectation, grasping at higher realizations and spiritual power, you cannot remain calm and relaxed. Therefore, you cannot grow; you cannot discover universal wisdom. So don't expect something big to happen; don't expect to receive spiritual realizations. Instead, try to generate simultaneously as much wisdom and pure motivation as you can and the enthusiastic feeling, "This is so worthwhile. Here I am, twenty, thirty, forty years old, and so far my entire life has been completely dedicated to attachment, to myself, to my I, but for the next five days, like a flash of lightning on a pitch black night, I have the chance to totally dedicate my life to others, with no expectation of anything for myself. I am so lucky." Be satisfied with that. "I'm surprised at myself. After all those decades in total darkness, possessed by attachment, not dedicating even one day of my life to all sentient beings, here I am suddenly dedicating the next five days of my life to others. It's like a flash of lightning, but it's enough for me. I'm satisfied. This is my meditation; this is my meditation course." Dwell in this enthusiastic feeling.

"At the same time, I'm observing intently the way attachment comes into my mind. Like an alert sentry, rifle at the ready, watching for the enemy, my wisdom sentry, totally conscious every moment, is observing intently and investigating how attachment arises."

Our normal, discriminating mind, our gross-level conception, or perception, is split. It is not an integrated mind. We have a way to treat that mind, a method to release it—a breathing exercise that makes space for wisdom and gets rid of the mundane, gross-level thinking that preoccupies your mind and makes it impossible for you to relax.

Meditation on the breath

First sit cross-legged, in the lotus or half-lotus position if you can, or just comfortably. Make sure your mind is here with your body. It's no good if your body is here but your mind's at home. You can't take a meditation course with your body alone. Meditation is done by the mind. Therefore, your mind should be with you in the present, not obsessed with another time, place, person or some other object. The method we use to bring attention totally to the here and now is concentration on the breath—focusing on how your breath moves through your nervous system.

This is not all that this method is helpful for; it has many other benefits. It can even help you recover from physical illness. For example, if your nervous system has been damaged by a stroke, intensive concentration on the movement of your breath through your nervous system can restore its function. This is experience, not just empty talk.

If you are unfamiliar with the following meditation, you might find it easier to concentrate by occluding the nostril you are *not* focusing on with your index finger.

As you breathe out through your left nostril, use your finger to block the right. Exhale slowly; don't rush it. Breathe normally, but make sure to exhale completely. Then, move your finger to block the left nostril as you inhale slowly and deeply through your right. Then, for a second time, block your right nostril while you exhale slowly, gently, naturally and completely through the left, and then block your left nostril as you again inhale slowly and completely through the right. Repeat all this for a third time. Thus, you exhale through the left and inhale through the right three times.

Then reverse the procedure, breathing out through the right and in through the left three times. While doing this, sit up straight. This keeps your nervous system straight and allows the air you inhale to pervade your whole body, your entire nervous system. If you don't keep your spine straight when you meditate, it is difficult for the breath energy to spread throughout your nervous system. Nevertheless, do this practice very naturally. Don't force it.

When you inhale, feel that the air completely fills your body, and when you exhale, feel that it completely leaves. But while you're doing this, don't sit there thinking, "Now I'm doing the breathing exercise." That's not necessary. Just do it, concentrating on the movement of the breath energy through your nervous system as much as you possibly can.

Also, don't think that this meditation is ridiculously simple. If you are aware, you will notice that people who are emotionally or mentally disturbed—for example, those who are depressed—breathe differently from normal people. This shows that the way the breath energy moves through the nervous system is very closely connected with the mind. You know from your own experience that when you are angry you don't breathe normally. Sometimes anger can even make you physically sick.

You can measure scientifically how many times a day you breathe in and out. Buddhism has also calculated this. If you train yourself in the breathing meditation and practice breathing in and out slowly every day, you can prolong your life. If air enters your nervous system in a disturbed way it can disturb your mind. You should breathe slowly, steadily, naturally and completely, like a reliable old clock ticking away. Your breath is like an internal clock.

After you have breathed out through the left and in through the right three times, and out through the right and in through the left three times, breathe in and out through both nostrils together. Again, bring the air in slowly, gently, naturally and completely, allowing it to fill your nervous system, and slowly, gently and completely send it out again. If your belt is too tight, loosen it. You should be comfortable when you do this practice. Again, don't think, "I am doing the breathing exercise...right nostril...left nostril...." Just let your mind dwell in the concentration. Breathe in and out through both nostrils together about twenty times.

After this, change your object of concentration from the breath to the feelings in your body. As the breath travels down through your nose and throat and into your heart and lungs, be aware of your bodily sensations. With each breath, your bodily sensations change. Be aware of those changes but don't intellectualize; just feel the nature of those sensations. In this way you can realize that changes in sensation and feeling are not a matter of intellect or belief but come automatically.

If your knees hurt, instead of allowing your gross mind to be preoccupied with the pain, seek out and observe its nature. You can try sending joy from your heart into your knees; perhaps the pain will disappear. Anyway, you should know that whenever pain or any other uncomfortable feeling arises, it is not permanent—it's there one minute, gone the next. Such feelings come and go minute by minute. Physical feelings are transitory; they never last. Just relax, watching how your body reacts to physical feelings and how your mind reacts when they arise. Don't intellectualize. Relax and let go. Be conscious and aware. How does the feeling arise? When does it come?

Between sessions

This is what you do during the meditation session; you integrate your energy. But when the session finishes and you go outside, don't squander all this effort by allowing your old, unconscious, preoccupied-by-sense-objects mind to arise. That's really a waste of time.

In the breaks between meditation sessions, Tibetan lamas try to maintain a session-like level of awareness. No matter what they are doing—eating, drinking, talking—they try to be totally conscious of what they are thinking, doing and saying. Of course, during a retreat it's much better to maintain silence. That makes it easier to observe and be aware of the nature of your sensations, which is the purpose of this exercise. This discipline is not easy but really most worthwhile.

For example, when you drink tea, drink consciously. Be totally aware of the feeling of the tea as it touches your tongue and passes down your throat, through your chest and into your stomach.

So keep as silent as possible, except for discussion groups, when you can share your experiences with others. Group discussion is serious investigation; an important part of this course. You help yourself and others—your Dharma friends. Totally dedicate yourselves to helping each other. This, too, is part of training the mind.

Whatever you discuss, do it with much compassion and with the intention of discovering your inner nature and human potential. Employ skillful wisdom and clear logic. This kind of conversation is much more worthwhile than our usual gossip, where we discuss pleasures of the senses and other trivial matters. Such conversations are useless. They lack substance and not only have no lasting benefit but also cause future confusion. Dharma discussions, on the other hand, are really worthwhile.

That's enough from me for today. Now let's take a break. In the next session, practice the breathing meditation I have just described. Thank you so much. Thank you very much. Thank you.

··· 2 ···

Techniques for the Meditation Session and the Break

THINK, "Why is my uncontrolled mind so strongly tied to this uncontrolled body? Why has my uncontrolled mind been associated with this sense-driven body for such a long time? It seems that my entire internal environment is totally agitated. When I was a child, I used other people; I made them work to take care of me, of my body. Now that I've grown, I myself have to expend great effort just to keep this body alive. Even such a simple thing as getting a job can be so difficult. If I didn't have this uncontrolled body, I wouldn't even need a job. And because of the association of uncontrolled body and mind, I'm tied to the tiny atoms of my material existence. All these problems come from the deep root of attachment and ego mind. My ego binds me to conditions and gives me no chance to experience internal peace, freedom and joy."

While I'm speaking, check what I'm saying; practice analytical meditation. Instead of allowing your senses to be preoccupied with other objects, pay full attention to what I'm saying and contemplate its meaning. Don't listen to Dharma with the attitude of a child in school.

If you cannot control your body for a short time—even an hour—if you cannot relax physically, your nervous system will not be relaxed. If your nervous system is not relaxed, your mind will not be relaxed and that will prevent you from seeing reality or experiencing inner peace. When your mind is relaxed, your nervous system becomes the kind of spacious, peaceful environment that knowledge-wisdom needs to grow. You don't have to strain yourself; there is a gentler method.

Even when your knee hurts, it's not as bad as you think—your ego exaggerates the pain. It solidifies the feeling, makes it feel unchangeable, like iron. This is a totally wrong conception, a completely unrealistic interpretation. If you can realize this, the pain will be digested by your wisdom and disappear. Why? Because the pain you feel in your knee does not arise by itself but in combination with ego activity. When one of these elements disappears, the combination also disappears.

You don't have to exert yourself to enjoy good meditation. Simply close your eyes, relax completely, and let your mind just watch. Don't expect bad thoughts to arise; don't expect good ones either. Just let go and observe how thoughts come, how thoughts go; how pain comes, how pain goes; how the agitated mind comes, how it goes. Just watch. Check up, "Where is this agitation I feel?" "What is this agitation I'm experiencing?" When you check up with analytic wisdom, agitation automatically disappears. It goes away by itself because agitation is neither flesh nor bone; it is not a physical thing. Agitation is just an expression of mind.

When you meditate, ignore your sense perceptions; don't pay attention to sights, sounds, smells, tangibles or tastes. Keep your eyes lightly closed; the meditating mind is not sense perception. Sense perception is blind; it is not an intelligent mind. Let your mind be totally open and aware.

When your mind reaches beyond pain, let it rest there.

When you focus your attention on the subjective mind that feels, the object of the feeling disappears. Let your mind remain there; don't concentrate on the feeling itself.

The wandering mind

If your mind gets distracted by external objects, focus on your breath. Breathe in deeply and completely through your nose, bringing your breath energy all the way down below your stomach to your navel. Push down gently with your diaphragm. Then tighten the muscles around your sex chakra—your internal, lower pelvic muscles. Draw the energy up from below and feel it meet the energy you have pushed down from above at a point about four fingers' breadth below the level of your navel and hold your breath. Touch that point with your finger to bring your mind's attention to that precise spot. Feel a joyful sensation there. Your mind will automatically focus on that point. Concentrate on that sensation.

When you do this meditation, hold your breath for as long as is comfortable, then exhale naturally, slowly and completely, but leave your mind concentrated on feeling.[2]

Do this five times. Breathe in; push down a little; hold your breath below the navel; tighten the lower muscles; feel the energy rise from below to meet the energy from above; focus your concentration there, just below your navel.

When these two energies meet at that point just below your navel they generate a kind of electrical energy. Light radiates from there and spreads throughout your entire nervous system.

Without grasping, feel totally blissful. Concentrate on that feeling of bliss. Unify your mind with bliss. Let your mind sink into that feeling; don't feel separate from it by thinking, "I am feeling blissful."

---

[2] Here Lama is referring to the mental factor of feeling as one of the meditation objects of the four foundations of mindfulness—mindfulness of body, feeling, mind and phenomena. You can simply remain in mindful awareness on feeling or engage in analysis of it: is it pleasant, unpleasant or neutral? Is it permanent or impermanent? And so forth. See *Practicing Wisdom*, Chapter 9, for Shantideva's approach to meditating on selflessness via the four mindfulnesses.

The dull mind

If your mind gets sluggish or sleepy, try to focus on the light energy just below your navel; visualize it getting clearer, brighter and more radiant. Your foggy mind will disappear. The view of the foggy, sluggish mind tends to be dark. When you visualize light, the sluggish mind automatically disappears. This is not just some hallucination. There's already electric light energy within your body. When the air energy pushed down from above mingles with the energy pulled up from below, that electric light is activated.

This is not religious dogma; it's scientific experience. Inhale slowly and deeply; bring the breath energy all the way down below your navel; push down a little; tighten the lower muscles; bring the energy up from below to meet the energy from above, just below the navel. From that point, electric light energy radiates throughout your entire nervous system—into your heart, your throat, your brain; into your legs, knees and feet. Feel the total unity of the electric light energy. Dwell in that blissful feeling of unity and light.

When you meditate, keep your mouth gently closed. Breathe only through your nose.

Session breaks

When it's time to break, get up from your seat slowly, with awareness. When you walk, link your fingers gently in front of you instead of letting your arms swing all over the place. Relax, but walk with awareness of your feelings. Go to the toilet or do whatever you have to do and return with awareness of your feelings. It's all meditation. Walking is meditation; sitting down is meditation. Everything becomes meditation. Meditation does not necessarily mean sitting in some corner, doing nothing. Your walking can be totally conscious; that, too, is meditation.

Now take a break as I've described. Return slowly. Pay attention to your inner feelings but don't forget the blissful feeling below your navel.

[Session break]

Don't expect your concentration on feeling to be perfect, like hitting a nail on the head.

Externally, relax. Internally, be mindful. When a distracting thought arises, watch with penetrating, mindful wisdom how your ego mind identifies this thought, how it reacts. Be fully aware. When the thought object disappears, let your mind rest without thoughts.

When the memory of a past, pleasurable experience arises, observe mindfully how your ego mind identifies this thought, how it grasps at it.

Instead of rejecting this memory, just allow yourself to feel. When you try to feel, the memory will digest itself and simply disappear. When your mind reaches beyond grasping at the memory of this pleasant experience, just let it stay there.

When the memory of a past, unpleasant experience arises, perhaps bringing guilt or depression, watch with mindful wisdom. Observe how your ego mind rejects this experience.

You can see that instead of facing the feeling of this bad experience and wanting to know its nature, your ego mind immediately wants to escape from it.

When the ego mind sees a desirable experience, it is magnetically drawn towards it—but it doesn't want to investigate the reality of that experience. When a bad experience arises, the ego mind immediately wants to run away. To the ego mind, even one minute of bad experience can feel like a year. According to the nature of that experience, such reactions are unrealistic, but for countless lives we have accumulated the imprints of such reactions in our mind. Therefore, our minds are unbalanced, out of equilibrium and automatically agitated. We call such minds dualistic—they make judgments according to superficial imagination rather than actual reality.

The ego mind paints its own picture onto reality and we then judge "good" or "bad" on the basis of this hallucination. Our ego mind cheats us by projecting its own hallucinated view of reality, in which we believe.

If your mind reaches beyond the memory of either bad or good experiences, let it dwell in that state and let go.

Thus, you can see that the guilty mind is a manifestation of ego, not wisdom.

You don't have to strain to control your mind. Just be wise; try to understand and identify how your ego functions. With understanding, control comes automatically and your mind becomes healthy and happy. Control of the mind is a natural thing, not artificial.

During session breaks, try to remain as mindful as possible. Even if you love your friend, be wise. Check whether your chatter helps your friend or not; will that conversation make your friend truly happy? If the answer is yes, of course, talk away. But be wise. Ask yourself how you want to help your friend; try to determine the best way of helping. Don't think, "If I don't talk to her, she'll freak out." What freaks out is the silly mind, the ego. The realistic mind won't freak out. That's good. Let the ego freak out. Then you'll easily recognize it.

Isn't what I'm saying true? We always want to help our friend, but usually our ignorant mind only makes our friend more agitated; instead of helping, we disturb. Therefore, be especially careful in retreat. If you want to discuss some disturbing mind for the purpose of psychological treatment, it is obviously worthwhile to talk, but if you just want to engage in some emotional conversation, it's a waste of time.

Thus, session breaks become a kind of session. It depends on your mind. Session breaks can definitely become meditation sessions and it's most worthwhile for you to try to make them so.

In Tibet, we always used to emphasize how important it was to be careful not to allow old habits to surface during the session break. Otherwise, it's like trying to clean a room by simply pushing the dirt from one side to the other. If you remain mindful during the break, when the next session starts you can go straight into your meditation without any distraction.

Thank you so much. Thank you very much. Thank you. Thank you.

Vajrapani Institute, 1983

· · · 3 · · ·

Give Your Ego the Wisdom Eye

I F YOUR EGO is obviously giving you trouble, reciting the mantra of Lord Buddha can help. Mantra is inner sound; therefore, when you recite a mantra verbally, you can feel it vibrating in your heart at the same time. As it does so, it digests and controls your ego's energy force.

The connotation of Lord Buddha's mantra is, "Control, great control, greatest control."[3] Recite it three times and then stop and listen silently to the inner sound of the mantra in your heart.

TA YA THA OM MUNÉ MUNÉ MAHAMUNAYÉ SOHA

TA YA THA OM MUNÉ MUNÉ MAHAMUNAYÉ SOHA

TA YA THA OM MUNÉ MUNÉ MAHAMUNAYÉ SOHA

When you realize through your own experience how the powerful energy force of your ego comes and goes, you will realize that as well as

---

[3] At other times Lama has explained that these controls mean (a) control over the causes of the suffering of the lower realms; (b) complete control over the delusions and karma that prevent liberation; and (c) control over self-cherishing and the subtle dualistic mind, which prevent enlightenment.

your physical body there exists another, different kind of energy—your mind.

Instead of fearfully running away when confronted by the energy force of your ego, it is better to stand up to it with wisdom. Face up to ego problems with wisdom. The narrow mind, the mind weak in wisdom, cannot face the problems ego brings.

Fulfilling your human potential

You can discover through your own experience that when you investigate with introspective knowledge-wisdom the way in which your ego functions, it disappears. That small experience gives you confidence that you have the power and the potential to discover egolessness, the basic nature of the human mind. You may not have truly realized egolessness, but your experience shows the logical possibility of doing so. You can see that you possess wisdom and intelligence and are not hopeless by nature. It is extremely worthwhile for you to gain that understanding.

Basically, your mind is weak. You don't comprehend that you have the potential to realize something like eternal peace. It doesn't even occur to you. However, a small experience of egolessness will give you a logical reason for generating the brave, courageous mind that strives for such heights of human attainment. Such understanding does not come from the wisdom or the power of the lamas. It comes from your own wisdom, the power of your own mind.

Realizing egolessness

We always use the word "ego," but although we're constantly saying "ego, ego, ego," we have no idea of the psychological nature of the ego or the way it controls our mind. We seem to think the ego is some kind of physical entity. Therefore, it is crucial to discover that the ego is not physical but mental.

Our lives are short; we do not have much time to realize egolessness, but striving to do so is what differentiates us from animals. Otherwise, how are we different? Animals enjoy the sense world and lead their lives to the best of their ability. Just like ourselves, they like those who feed them and dislike those who beat them. What's the difference?

Perhaps you think, "Rubbish! I can conceptualize, I can write; I can make money to support and enjoy my life." But even rats and mice can look after themselves with ego and attachment. They can collect and store food many times their own weight. What about bees? Even though their lives are so short, they collect enough honey to last for maybe hundreds of years. What, then, is the difference between bees and so-called intelligent humans if the mental attitude is the same, where both are living only for sense pleasure? Perhaps bees are even more intelligent than we are—they live such short lives but accumulate vast amounts of what gives them pleasure.

Therefore, I think it's extremely important that while we occupy these precious human bodies, where intelligence and many other good qualities have come together, we take this opportunity to seek our inner nature and release ourselves from all the problems of mental defilement, which come from our ego. From the time we were born, everything we've done has come from our ego, but whatever pleasure we've experienced has been so transitory and small. Nevertheless, don't think, "Oh, I'm too bad; my mind is completely dominated by my ego." Don't put yourself down. Instead, be happy to realize what's happening.

Guiding yourself

To realize that only your own mind and effort can release you from your ego is most worthwhile. For years and years, all you've done is build up your ego, and under the influence of its hallucinated projection of the sense world, you've run, run, run from one thing to another, as if you'd lost your mind. To now have even a flash of recognition of this reality is most worthwhile and well worth the effort. Don't think that without your own effort, without using your own wisdom, you can stop the schizophrenic mental problems that result from the energy force of your own ego. It's impossible.

No lama believes that he can solve your problems without your own effort and action. That's a dream. If that's what you think, it's a complete misconception. "God will do everything for me; Buddha will do everything for me. I'll just wait." That's not true either. "I don't have to do anything." That's just not true. You've already done everything and now you have to experience the powerful consequences. You can see all this through your own experience. Just one meditation session is all it takes.

What I would like is for each of you to become a wise human being instead of one dominated by the energy force of a super-sensitive ego. At the end of this meditation course, I'd like you to be thinking, "Well, that was my own meditation course, given by my own wisdom." If you feel like that, the course was worthwhile, but if you go around telling people, "This high Tibetan lama gave a meditation course; I was there," it's just another ego trip. What's the purpose? Your old habits, your schizophrenic mental attitudes, haven't changed a bit. So what was the meditation that you did? Lord Buddha is already enlightened. Through his own effort, with his own wisdom, he freed himself from the schizophrenic mind, but here we are, still agitated and confused.

Realization is highly personal. It depends upon each individual's mind, effort and wisdom. Realization is completely individual. Even though you're all meditating on the same thing, from morning to night, each of you has different experiences according to the level of your own mind.

If you think, "Oh, I have so much to do at home...my house, my family, my friends...it's difficult to sit and meditate," it means your mind is ensnared by the worldly life. You've been like that from the time you were born until now, and if you keep going that way, you'll end up dying with nothingness. If this is how you live, how will you ever finish anything? In the materialistic life, work continues to pile up—one thing after another, then another, another, another—and you never reach the point where you can say, "Ah, at last I've finished everything; now I can sit and meditate." That time will never come.

When your mind is occupied by ego energy, it's like constantly having needles stuck into your body. That would be pretty uncomfortable, wouldn't it? Being under the control of ego is exactly the same. Thus, you can realize how important it is to release attachment and ego. If you can manage to do so, you will realize everlasting joy, inner freedom, inner liberation, nirvana…it doesn't matter what you call it.

By realizing the agitated nature of his ego department, Tibet's great yogi Milarepa fled to the mountains. There, eating only nettles, he lived like an animal, but his mind was much happier and he had far greater pleasure than before. You can be eating three meals a day and still think that your life is too ascetic. If you were sent to live like Milarepa, you'd freak out: "Oh, that's his trip, not mine." Maybe you'd worry that if everybody were to live like Milarepa, there'd be nobody left to eat all that supermarket food and it would go to waste. Don't worry about the supermarket; if you retreat to the mountains, the supermarket will come to you.

Learning from all phenomena

For those seekers investigating the nature of inner reality, problems help; instead of harming, problems benefit them. Problems give them more energy, greater wisdom and deeper realizations. Negative experiences become positive. They don't even see such experiences as negative but as opportunities to learn.

For example, there's another story from the life of Milarepa. After many years' study with his guru, Marpa, Milarepa was sent back to visit the village where he was born. "Go back home," said Marpa. "Something will happen." When Milarepa finally reached his old house, it was completely deserted, dilapidated and occupied by wild animals and birds. At first he was a bit shocked, but the experience became a teaching—he realized the inevitability of decay.

Also, all villagers were afraid to go near Milarepa's old house. Even after his mother died, everybody avoided it because they were afraid of his black magic. In fact, when Milarepa first got back nobody recognized him, and when he asked about the house, the neighbors said, "We're too scared to go near it because that's where the black magician Milarepa used to live." Milarepa learned from such experiences; he saw deeper into the nature of reality.

Anyway, slowly, slowly, he went to the house and saw how derelict it had become. But even though his mother had died long ago, all the family possessions were still there because nobody had dared to touch them. As he looked around, he saw some old bones lying in the mud on the floor. When he picked them up he realized they were his mother's. This, too, became a great teaching for him; he saw clearly the impermanent nature of all phenomena. He didn't need anyone to tell him, "All things are impermanent." He realized it clearly for himself.

We, however, do not see the world as clearly as Milarepa did. Because of the way our ego interprets things, we see the sense world as solid, self-existent, concrete. Those who have realized impermanence see it completely differently. They see the world changing automatically hundreds of times a minute. You can understand this yourself by watching your mind in meditation. You can see how your internal world—the feelings and sensations that continually rise and fall in your mind—change automatically from moment to moment. That inner expression of impermanence is similar to what is happening in the external world.

Exploring your internal world

Actually, watching your internal world is much more interesting than watching a movie and certainly more worthwhile. Once you've seen a movie, you don't want to see it again; you get bored the second time. But if you watch your mind with skillful wisdom you will never get bored. Every minute, there's something new. Your mind is constantly moving. It's a remarkable experience.

Every time your ego contacts an object, its interpretation leaves a different imprint on your consciousness. Those imprints react again and again. That's what we call karma—cause and effect. The imprints are the cause; the reaction is the effect. That's karma. Therefore we say that karma is very powerful. Why? Because the *imprints* left by previous ego activity are very powerful; extremely strong.

The energy force of ego bursts into your mind without permission. Even if you don't want it to enter it forces its way in. If someone were to rush into your house without knocking you'd get really upset, wouldn't you? "What's going on? You didn't even knock!" Even if your closest friend comes in without knocking you're likely to object. So isn't it silly that when the negative energy force of ego walks uninvited into your mind, instead of getting upset you say, "Welcome, ego. Please come in. How are you? Have a cup of tea. Would you like some chocolate?"

All we ever do is try to please our ego; it's like we're always paying homage to our ego, offering it tea, chocolate and prayers. We dedicate all our energy to our ego and what do we get in return? What does our ego offer us? Mental pollution. It brings such a foul, suffocating smell in our minds that there's hardly room to breathe.

So from now on, instead of welcoming your ego's energy force, stand guard against it with mindfulness and wisdom, watching with penetrative attention for the first sign of its arrival. And when it comes, instead of greeting it warmly, "How are you, ego? Come right in," examine it with a great big wisdom eye—a wisdom eye bigger than your head. Just watch it. When you give your ego the wisdom eye it disappears all by itself.

Mental continuity

In the next meditation session, I would like you to check how your mind of today is related to the experiences of yesterday's ego games. Check; observe. How are they linked? Similarly, check back to last week; last month; last year. Go all the way back through your life. Check with your big wisdom eye how your ego and attachment have functioned over the years; how you have identified things at different ages; how you have perceived different views, all of which have been projections of your own ego.

If your mind were not connected with last year's ego, there'd be no reason for memories to keep coming back uncontrollably into your mind. Therefore, check how these experiences relate to the continuity of mind. Go back as far as your time in the womb. Forgetting previous experiences and clinging to the future is not realistic. Unless you have psychic power, you have no idea whether you'll be alive next year or not. Nobody can guarantee you that. And you don't have to be sick to die. One minute you can be well, drinking a cup of tea; the next minute, you're dead. We all know that this can happen; we've seen it. We're not babies.

If you check well enough you'll find that even when you were in your mother's womb you experienced ego and attachment. Check where that came from. It didn't come from itself; it had to come from something else. There is no such self-existent entity that doesn't depend on something else—for example, a permanent soul. There is no such thing as a permanent soul, ego, consciousness or mind of attachment; nor is there any self-existent physical entity, either. Belief in such things is a wrong conception. Some religions, like Hinduism or Christianity, talk of an eternal soul. That's a misconception. They have no understanding of the characteristic nature of the soul. Impermanent means changing every moment. How could there be a permanent, never-changing soul? It's impossible. If you accept the existence of a permanent soul, you have to accept the existence of a permanent human being. It's impossible for there to be a permanent human being. Where is that person?

Therefore, in the next session, check back through all your experiences of how your mind has perceived the sense world from when you were in your mother's womb up to now. Check its different interpretations, its different feelings. You will find this meditation very helpful in integrating your mind and life and introducing a little order into both.

Begin the meditation by concentrating single-pointedly on the movement of your breath and the feelings in your body. Then move on to an analytical meditation, checking your experiences as I've just described. When you find an object, or experience, on which you want to focus, practice placement meditation—concentrate single-pointedly on that object. In Sanskrit, this kind of meditation is called *samadhi*. Keep your mind on the memory of that experience for as long as you can. When your mind begins to get distracted by other thoughts, repeat your analytical meditation until you get to that point again and re-focus your attention upon it.

Now it's time to stop. Start the next session with questions and answers with Dr. Nick and then do the meditation I've just described. Questions and answers are good. Be open; just say whatever you think. Don't have any expectations. Don't worry, "Perhaps I'll ask a stupid question. Perhaps Dr. Nick will freak out; he mightn't like my question." I guarantee he won't freak out. Whether you agree or disagree, just speak your mind. It's most worthwhile. Our discussions are not for some material purpose; we're searching for what's best for the human mind. Also, when you ask questions you're not trying to find answers for yourself alone but for the benefit of all.

Furthermore, when different people in the group express themselves you hear a wide range of opinions, which can only help to deepen everybody's understanding. It's almost like psychotherapy, group psychotherapy. We're working together with compassion to solve everybody's problems and help each other. You also ask the group leader questions out of compassion—to help him destroy his misconceptions. We all have misconceptions. Therefore, don't worry.

Thank you so much. Thank you.

Vajrapani Institute, 1983

· · · 4 · · ·

Your Mental Bureaucracy

I N A WAY, you people are intellectually very strong. That's good, because Buddhism is also very strong. It's like a knife in your ego—when you meditate, your ego comes out. Therefore, many people feel that Lama's approach to the mind is not a simple thing. I agree; it can be quite difficult. I make you work hard, don't I? But when *you* work, when *you* deal with your own problems and recognize the way your ego reacts, it's really most worthwhile.

I don't have to do it this way. I could easily present Buddhism to you very diplomatically; I could explain it with very sweet words. We could run this five-day course like a nightclub with a lot of nice words, dancing and fun. That's possible, but it's not the point. You've come here for the meditation, not the floor show. In fact, you've come here precisely because you already know all there is to know about the kind of fun you find in nightclubs.

Also, I don't want to joke around with you. We're all sick of the joking trip. For countless lives and from the time you were born until now all you've done is play games and joke around. What, then, is the point of coming to a retreat to joke around again, this time with a lama? It's a waste of your time and mine. Therefore, it's most worthwhile that *you* work. This is *your* course, not mine. If you feel, "This is my meditation course; I'm working; I'm alert, not sleeping," that's really worthwhile.

What makes your being here highly meaningful is if, through knowing the nature of the external nightclub—which only exhausts, conflicts and agitates you—you're here seeking the inner nightclub of everlasting joy. That's the perfect motivation for coming to this course—you're here trying to familiarize yourself with your mental attitude, with what's going on in your internal world, instead of ignoring what your ego is up to; you're trying to learn how to examine your own mind. In other words, you're studying to become your own psychologist, your own lama.

Not only are you people intellectually strong, you're also skeptical. That's good; Lord Buddha's teaching is skeptical too. This meeting of skeptics is excellent. Do you understand what I mean by skeptical? I mean you don't easily believe or accept anything; you check and experiment to see if something works or not. If it doesn't, you keep checking, checking, checking, using your brain, your wisdom. In that way, you grow. This is all part of the path of inner freedom, liberation and enlightenment. Believing emotionally, without understanding, what somebody teaches you has nothing to do with any religion, even though you might pretend, "I'm a such and such." It's just a label and still an ego trip.

Ego, attachment and impermanence

The two departments of ego and attachment work together in your mind, and as long as they do, whatever sense pleasure you enjoy, wherever you go, whatever friends you have, nothing lasts. Your ego makes a wrong projection on an object and your attachment follows without hesitation and gets completely stuck on, or tied to, that object. This splits and severely agitates your mind.

I'm sure you can philosophize intellectually that things are impermanent but if you check more deeply into how your ego interprets objects, what it projects onto them, you will find that it's expecting them to last, perceiving them as permanent.

When two people get married, their egos' interpretation is that they should be together forever, in life and even after death. It's so exaggerated. There's no way people can make that kind of decision. It's not up to them; it's up to karma. Uncontrollably, karmic energy decides which partner lives and which dies. And when one finally does, the other misses him or her badly and experiences tremendous suffering.

All that worry and weeping, missing and memory, comes from the two mental departments of ego and attachment. Not understanding the impermanent nature of phenomena and expecting to live happily ever after, as ego and attachment wish, brings the reaction of misery. That is a karmic result, or effect. If you understand impermanence there's no upset, no misery; you accept death as a natural thing. In fact, you expect it to happen. With understanding, there's no worry. You know separation is natural.

Therefore, instead of blindly following the grasping and attachment that result from the way your ego interprets things, it's better to renounce. Perhaps you think that when I say renounce I mean that you should get rid of all your possessions, but true renunciation isn't physical, it's mental. It doesn't refer to what things are worth monetarily but to how your mind values them. Your mind makes things seem very important because it does not see their reality and grossly overestimates their nature.

When you know that phenomena are changeable, transitory and impermanent by nature you expect things to disappear. Of course, as I just said, everybody knows this intellectually, but when you meditate on the sensations of your body and mind you *experience* their automatically-changing nature. That's not intellectual philosophy but personal experience. Other objects, such as your family and friends, material possessions, or whatever else may be your biggest object of attachment, are the same in nature. Everything is transitory, momentary; nothing lasts. We cling to these things because we think that they're helpful, but try to ascertain whether they really help or harm your mind. Perhaps instead of inducing peace of mind they prevent it. You check up.

Of course, it depends on your own mind. Generally speaking, the greater the number of objects of attachment around you the more your mind is split, agitated and disordered. That's natural; you check up. As long as the association of these two departments of ego and attachment occupies the mind, who can be happy? Even the richest man on Earth will be miserable if these two departments occupy his mind. Therefore, don't grasp too much at the future, imagining, "If only I had this, that and the other, I'd be happy. Oh, how I wish I had those things in my life." It's not true.

You can never be sure. To your ego's interpretation, a friend, husband or wife can only be of help. Your ego grasps, "My life would be so much better if only I had somebody." But think of a couple that stays together for, say, ten years, through countless ups and downs, pretending to be happy; maybe happy half the time and unhappy the rest. Even after all that, there's still much attachment. Then the husband dies and for the next ten years the wife is miserable. She suffers; she's lonely; she can't get him out of her mind. So what was actually worthwhile? She's spent ten years of her life building, building, building attachment, her ego pretending to be happy, happy, happy, and then, when her great object of attachment disappears, she gets another ten years of misery and worry. For ten years she's had the idea, "My husband helps my life," but did he really? Perhaps the only help she got from him was another ten years of misery.

Do you understand what I'm saying? I'm not talking about the outer reality but the psychological aspect—the way the two departments of ego and attachment function in the mind. That's what makes life difficult.

Renunciation

When you realize how absolutely unrealistic and silly these two departments are you'll see how silly you are to keep following that association. It's a psychological thing, not a matter of saying, "I have attachment to this object; I'd better get rid of it." That's not what I mean by renunciation. It's mind, not matter. Therefore, don't feel threatened that when I say "renounce" you're going to lose all your material possessions. You have to understand that Lord Buddha's renunciation is psychological.

In his Mahayana teachings Lord Buddha himself said, "If you have dedicated your body, speech and mind to the happiness of other sentient beings and have no attachment to your possessions, then even if you're a monk, you can own a thousand houses." If you are free of attachment you have no feeling that anything really belongs to you. But remember, this is psychological. After you get home from this meditation course don't throw all your furniture into the street: "Lama said I have too much attachment. I'd better get rid of all my stuff." If you don't understand what I'm talking about, it can be dangerous. Therefore, try to understand your own psychology—how the two departments of ego and attachment occupy your mind—as best you can.

If you gain this understanding, then even if you're surrounded by your family and friends, you won't grasp at them too much. It's natural. If I cling too strongly to a flower I'll crush it and destroy its beauty. Similarly, if a husband clings to and squeezes his wife she'll freak out and won't be able to stand it. Because of his great attachment—perhaps he's so jealous that he won't even let her walk down the street alone— she'll no longer see him as attractive. A husband or wife who doesn't cling and is natural, relaxed and free appears more beautiful to his or her spouse.

Therefore, be natural. Husbands and wives who love each other should not grasp at or squeeze their spouse with attachment but try to better understand the up and down nature of each other's mind and, on that basis, help and support each other. That's the way to bring beautiful, warm feelings into a relationship, which, as a result, will last longer.

Superstition

Under the control of completely unrealistic craving, grasping and attachment, from the time we were born until now we have totally dedicated the energy of our body, speech and mind to the pursuit of material possessions and sense pleasures and have no idea of how our mind reacts to these conceptions. We see only the façade; our limited mind cannot see below the surface. Attachment and ego are narrow, limited minds that don't see the entirety, only part.

Perhaps even now one of you is sitting here thinking, "I'm stuck here listening to this silly lama while perhaps back home somebody is stealing my wife" or "Maybe my boss is planning to fire me." Our minds create such worries. All this comes from attachment. We have so many fears, so many fantasies. Perhaps your fantasy becomes so real that when you get back home you beat your wife: "I'm sure you cheated on me." We're so unrealistic; we fantasize and worry, "Perhaps this will happen; maybe I'll lose that." All this expectation and superstition is very strong, causes much mental suffering and remains in our mind for a long time.

If somebody beats you up you get really upset but a beating lasts only a short time. The worrying mind beats you up day after day, week after week, month after month, year after year, and lifetime after lifetime. Even now you're completely under its control. You think you're free, but you're not.

Therefore you have to determine, "Dharma wisdom is the only solution to my problems; the only vehicle that can carry me to everlasting happiness. Only Dharma can truly save me from danger. Any minute, I could lose my mind and go mad. It's possible; I've already created the cause for this to happen. Dharma wisdom, understanding the nature of the mind, is my only protection. It can accompany me all the time." You cannot rely on material things.

For example, when husbands and wives are apart they worry about each other and feel agitated and insecure. Dharma wisdom, however, is always with you and makes you happy. Material things, the things you think your life depends on, are unreliable—sometimes with you, sometimes not. Also, psychologically, material possessions can become your worst enemy. When you're dying and have to leave them, you feel miserable. The more you have, the worse you feel. Check up right now. You can see that your mind is drawn towards whatever your attachment has labeled "good." Check up in meditation. Therefore, at the time of death, when you know that you're losing forever everything that you possess, all these things simply serve to make you more agitated. That worried mind itself almost kills you. Your elements are already completely out of balance; the mental shock of losing all your possessions delivers the final blow.

Dying without attachment

When Tibetan lamas knew they were going to die they'd give away all their possessions. In the months or years preceding their death they'd donate all their books to the monastery, their money to the poor and so forth because they knew that if their mind were to get stuck on an object of attachment at the time of death it would only cause suffering and prevent them from dying freely.

As I mentioned before, attachment has nothing to do with the material value of an object. It's not like the more expensive something is the greater your attachment to it and the cheaper it is the less your attachment. It's not like that. You can be strongly attached to even a piece of paper. It doesn't depend on its outer valuation. Ego and attachment are what give things their value.

Why am I telling you this? Because you might think that poor people don't have attachment; that Himalayan peasants who own nothing but a cow have less attachment than wealthy Westerners, which is not true. Attachment doesn't depend on what others think something is worth; it depends on the mind. For example, chickens have strong attachment to where they live; a chicken thinks its coop is the best place in the world. That's the way its ego works. It's the mind.

You probably think I'm exaggerating, but I'm not. Remember, ego and attachment don't work at the intellectual level. If you ask a chicken on its roost if it's happy it's not going to reply, but intuitively, a chicken feels happy in familiar surroundings. If something intrudes it gets angry and tries to drive the trespasser away. If we behave in the same way we're no better than chickens; nevertheless, if somebody invades our space we get just as upset as they do. What's the difference?

Also, under the power of its ego, a chicken eats hundreds of insects every day. We, too, use the power of our ego to try to control or take advantage of others. All this comes from attachment, not from our basic human nature, which is pure and can be developed infinitely.

Satisfaction

Remember this when you meditate. Concentrate on the feelings in your body and mind and when you get distracted, observe the role attachment plays. This method will show you the true nature of your own mind. Because of the way in which your attachment reacts to how your ego interprets things, you're not happy when trying to attain perfect concentration and get agitated and distracted when you meditate.

You think rich people are very lucky and wish you had their wealth, but if you understood human psychology, the nature of the mind and how attachment works, you wouldn't care. Who cares about external wealth? In my opinion, the truly rich person is the one who has a satisfied mind. Satisfaction is real wealth and you can keep it forever. The affluence of satisfaction comes from understanding knowledge-wisdom, not from external things.

For example, we can eat and drink the most expensive things but still feel dissatisfied while a chicken can eat the most terrible garbage and go to sleep content. Satisfaction comes from the mind. We can't believe how a chicken could possibly sleep after eating dirt so horrible that it would make us sick, but the chicken fills its stomach and goes to sleep satisfied. Satisfaction comes from the mind, not from food or any other material object.

Otherwise, where does super-satisfaction come from? Where on Earth can you find super-satisfactory beauty or pleasure? Sydney? New York? Paris? Where? It's nowhere, non-existent. There is no external shape, color or form on Earth that itself can produce super-satisfaction. Just because there are supermarkets doesn't mean you can find super-satisfaction in them. Sometimes all you'll find there is more dissatis-faction.

Therefore, when you meditate, take a serious look at what causes sat-isfaction. Check deeply and come to a firm conclusion. Don't be wishy-washy, "Maybe, maybe, maybe...." Check thoroughly, again and again; analyze, investigate and bring every thought to a logical conclusion.

Finally, make a determination, integrating all your trains of thought into one definite conclusion. That's the way to do analytical meditation. The vacillating mind is split. You need to integrate your mind by coming to a definite conclusion.

What you need to decide once and for all is: "I'm tired of being a servant to my ego. My ego rules my mind and even though it continuously gives me nothing but trouble and no time for rest, I still spend my entire life as its servant. My mind is constantly in turmoil only because of my ego. I'm not going to be a slave to my ego any longer!"

All the worry we experience comes from the two departments of ego and attachment. For example, we all want a beautiful body but at the same time our sneaky, grasping attachment makes us eat more than our body requires and we get fat. This is just a simple example but it's one to which most of us can relate.

Check it out for yourself. You need little food but your attachment to over-eating makes you heavy and uncomfortable. At the same time, you want to be attractive. These two things are in conflict. Which do you choose—your ego's wish for a beautiful body or your attachment to eating food? Look into your mind; find the one to which you cling the most. One mind is there, grasping at beauty; the other is there too, knowing that if you eat too much you'll get fat and destroy whatever beauty you have. Still, you can't stop eating. These two minds agitate you. Psychologically, they beat you up, but despite their constant mashing, you still keep saying "Yes, yes, yes…."

It's very funny. The human mind is so weird…and very silly, if you really check. The idea that thin is beautiful and fat is ugly comes from the mind. Of course, I agree that if you are too fat it can be unhealthy;

that's OK. But the idea, the picture, created by attachment and desire of what is beautiful and what is ugly is so silly, isn't it? It's not the reality of the fat that bothers you but the idea that it's unattractive. Why? Because you cling to reputation; you're worried what other people will think of you.

I tell you, mother sentient beings on this Earth are so silly. People in one country think something is pretty; people in another country think the same thing is ugly. Here, this is bad; there, it is good. To some, this is beautiful; to others something else is beautiful. It's all made up; they're just different ideas.

Beautiful and ugly

Otherwise, where is that external, permanent, absolute beauty? It is only the way our ego mind interprets objects that makes them beautiful or ugly. You check up; it's so simple. When you do the body-sweeping meditation—where your mind examines every part of your body—try to find the beauty. Check up: what's beautiful? Which part are you clinging to as beautiful? Check up. Your interpretation of what's beautiful and what's ugly is extremely superficial. It's just your ego's projection but it makes you very confused. You're confused even now. You no longer know what is good and what is bad. Really!

When you go to the bathroom you don't stand there admiring what you've just deposited into the toilet bowl, do you? Similarly, when you gaze into the mirror at your beautiful body or face, when you get stuck on the aspects of yourself that your ego's projection has deemed attractive, let your mind travel into your body from the inside of your nose all the way down, trying to determine exactly where your beauty is. You'll find that in essence, every part of your body is identical to what you've just excreted. This is scientific reality, not a matter of belief. The object of beauty that you cling to seems attractive simply because of an extremely superficial judgment made by your fickle mind.

Look at the confused young women of today. They run from one man to another, to another, to another; another man, another man, another man…they experience much trouble, more trouble, trouble on top of trouble, but at the same time they're expecting, "Maybe this is the one, maybe this is the one…." These are such superficial experiences, all mental projections painted by their egos. "Maybe this, maybe this," with expectation; "Maybe this, maybe this, maybe this…." No satisfaction at all; always trouble.

Perhaps you're thinking, "Oh, Lama's putting women down too much." Men are the same; they're so deluded. One changes his wife, superficially discriminating the new one as "Good, good, good…." Then after a while "good" turns to "bad," so he changes again. Then good, then bad, then change; then good, then bad, then change. His judgment—good and bad, beautiful and ugly—is completely super-ficial and has nothing whatsoever to do with reality, either inner or outer. There's no understanding, no communication, only fear and insecurity—all because of ego and attachment.

All this comes from the mind. We're totally preoccupied with our ego's superficial projections and turn our backs on reality. No wonder we're completely confused and unable to communicate properly with any living being. All this comes from our big ego.

Dedicate yourself to others

Therefore, it is highly worthwhile to switch your mental attitude from the attachment that always says "I, I, I" to purely dedicating your life to the welfare of others, as we tried to do at the beginning of this course. Recognize that for years and years you have been building attachment but still have nothing to show for it. It's really important to be aware of this. When you dedicate your life to others you acknowledge that true human beauty is not on the outside, not the view projected by your ego onto another person's skin, but rather others' inner potential. When you realize that, you will respect other sentient beings and try to help them, instead of respecting only yourself and spending all your time developing your two inner departments of ego and attachment.

Wherever you go—East, West, sky, earth, beneath the earth—there are other sentient beings. If, through having recognized the false conceptions of ego and attachment, you develop pure motivation and dedicate your life to others, your life will become truly worthwhile. You will give real meaning to being alive and your relationships with those around you will be much better.

You don't have to change anything external; the only change you have to make is within your mind. As soon as you change your projection, the outside world changes too; it changes automatically because your basic view becomes positive.

When Lord Buddha spoke of heaven and hell he was not referring to some place up in the sky or under the ground sitting there waiting for you. Such things do not exist. There is no permanent hell waiting somewhere for you to come and burn in; nor is there some permanent heaven waiting for you either. Whatever you see comes only from your mind. That's why Lord Buddha always emphasized the impermanent nature of suffering phenomena. Even if you personally killed everybody on Earth, there's no permanently existing hell waiting for you to come and suffer in forever. There's no such thing, even if you kill all sentient beings. There's no permanent suffering.

But there is such a thing as an impermanent mental reaction. When your knees hurt, they don't hurt forever but they do hurt for a while. Even though it's impermanent, you do feel pain. That, too, is in your mind; the pain in your knee comes from your mind. Check up. If you send a powerful blissful feeling into your knee, the pain will disappear. Of course, I can't say it has nothing to do with the conditions. Actually, it's a combination of the conditions and the mind, but your ego makes the pain hurt too much. If you change your attitude, the pain will go away. Therefore, it's an impermanent phenomenon.

Vajrapani Institute, 1983

Carol Royce-Wilder

··· 5 ···

Questions and Answers

WHEN YOU INVESTIGATE your mind, questions automatically arise. Instead of reacting negatively—"Oh, I have too many questions"—think, "How lucky I am to have questions. For such a long time I have accepted being under the control of ego and attachment without question. For once I am trying to understand and control my own internal world; therefore it's good to have questions."

When you ask questions, you get answers. Those answers become wisdom; questions produce understanding knowledge-wisdom.

Sometimes our weird mind thinks, "Normally, I have no questions; I'm happy. Now that I've been listening to Lama carrying on, I'm confused. I have so many questions. All I get from listening to Lama is questions." That's possible. When you're under the control of wrong conceptions and the superficial view, you have no questions, but when you begin to understand how your false conceptions and projections work, serious questions arise. That's worthwhile.

In America, there's some kind of telephone hot-line you can call if you have a question and need an answer right away, even if it's the middle of the night. Somebody showed it to me in New York. Other people can listen in. So I listened for a while; it was really funny. The answers the man on the end of the line gave were so silly. It was incredible; the things people asked and the answers they got were for me a completely new culture. But I enjoyed it very much. Afterwards I thought a lot about the questions and the answers. I kept asking myself, "What kind of mind is that?"

Anyway, during this retreat I should be giving each of you personal interviews, but you are too many and we don't have enough time. Therefore, if my talks have created any confusion or difficulty, now is the time to ask any questions that you might have.

Q. I find it very difficult to concentrate on only one thing. I have many distractions, both inner and outer, which are difficult to ignore, and I can't keep my meditation focused on the object of concentration.

Lama. I've addressed that already. Whenever distraction arises, whether it be a dog barking or the memory of some old experience, instead of reacting negatively and trying to force it out of your consciousness, just watch the thought—how it comes and goes. When you watch your thoughts with wisdom they disappear of their own accord. If you don't watch with wisdom, thoughts appear; if you watch with wisdom, they disappear. That's their nature. Once the distraction has gone you automatically revert to single-pointed attention on your object of concentration.

Another technique you can use with distracting thoughts is to see how you feel when they arise. Instead of looking at them like an outside observer, "Oh, what is that?" concentrate on feeling; pay more attention to how you feel. Examine how sense perception registers in your consciousness, how you interpret it and how you feel.

Q. How long do we hold our breath when we do the vase breathing exercise?

Lama. Start with what's comfortable, but do try to extend the period. At first you'll find it difficult to control your breath but it becomes easier with time. On inhalation, hold it for as long as you can but on exhalation, don't hold it out too long. Exhale naturally, slowly and completely, and once you have, again inhale naturally, slowly and completely—with strong concentration. If you do this properly, your mind and nervous system will automatically relax. They'll be calm and quiet. If your concentration is strong, you'll feel as if you've almost stopped breathing. That's the experience, although it takes time to reach that stage. But if you have excellent concentration, your breathing will be completely silent.

The first time new students meditate their breathing can be really noisy but with experience it gets quieter and more peaceful. The breathing meditation is a very useful technique to master because in our busy society, with work and everything else, it's very simple to take a moment and focus on your breath. Whether you're at work, in a restaurant or wherever, you can concentrate on the movement of your breath and your sensations. You don't need any other object of concentration. This is very helpful for integrating your mind.[4]

Q. I'm more distracted by shapes and colors than by discursive thought. I like to watch them. Are these really distractions?

Lama. It depends. If you remain concentrated on feeling but at the same

[4] For more teachings on vase breathing, see Lama Yeshe's *Becoming Vajrasattva*, p.40 ff., and *Bliss of Inner Fire*.

time get an impression of different shapes and colors passing by, that's not distraction. But if your mind moves away from the object of concentration and pays more attention to the shape or color, then at that time, yes, you're distracted. Just having an impression of something else in your mind is not necessarily a distraction.

Q. If my meditation is going well and I'm not getting distracted for long periods I get quite pleased with myself, but then I feel guilty about being pleased with myself. Is this just my ego?

Lama. Definitely. But you don't have to feel guilty about recognizing that your meditation is going well. Instead of feeling egocentric pride, dedicate your meditation to others. Then your ego won't arise. Think, "This meditation is for others. I'm not doing it because I'm obsessed with my own problems. I have dedicated my life to the welfare of others. Should I feel happy and joyful as a result, may my good behavior and positive actions make others feel good. This is my practice of charity." Offering your friends good instead of selfish behavior is most worthwhile; it helps other sentient beings. There's no pride involved in this. You want to create a positive environment for others; you want to give them a good visualization by improving yourself and becoming a good example. If you dedicate your meditation and other actions in that way there'll be no room for pride or ego. It's most necessary to do this.

Remember what I said at the beginning of the course: don't expect me to give you any big realizations in these five short days. I asked you to think, "Whatever happens during this course, I don't care. Recognizing how selfish I have been for countless lives, I dedicate the next five days to benefiting others." If you do that, no matter what I say, no matter what happens during the course, everything you do during these five days becomes powerfully positive. Thus you can see that whether your meditation becomes positive or negative depends on your own mind. I'm saying this for all of you, not just in reply to that question.

Q. If I enjoy things like food and music, is that the same as being attached to them, and if so, how do I stop the attachment?

Lama. You stop attachment by understanding what it is and how it works. When, for example, you realize how attachment grasps at more food than you need, it will stop naturally. You can't stop it by generating some kind of radical, rejecting mind. Understanding brings natural change; when you understand attachment to food, it will automatically change into detachment. Satisfaction has to do with the mind, not the amount of food you eat.

Also, listening to music isn't necessarily negative. That, too, depends on your mind. When you listen to music, analyze how the sound is produced, how it comes through your sense of ear and registers in your consciousness and how attachment clings to it. In that way, listening to music becomes analytical meditation and a form of wisdom.

Q. But if I hear some music that I like and just think that it's nice, is that different from attachment?

Lama. Yes, that can be different. But as I said, you have to know the basic nature of how the sound is generated, what kind of mind produces music and how your interest in it arises. If you understand the total nature of the music, it's impossible to be attached to it. Our problem is that we cling to it, wanting more, more, more. We don't understand the true nature of music, therefore we crave it. When we understand the nature of music our attitude becomes, when it's there, it's there; when it's not there, it's not there and we don't miss it terribly. It's the same with any other object of desire. When we understand the nature of the object and the nature of the subject—the mind of attachment—and the way they function, our attachment automatically falls away. If we don't have this understanding, attachment only makes us miserable.

Q. We're told that if we create negative karma we'll be reborn as some lower being. How can we really check up on this? You tell us not to simply believe what we are told, but how do we analyze this point?

Lama. It's not necessary to simply believe—through your own experience you can see the possibility of this happening. For example, you see people in human form whose minds and behavior are worse than those of animals. The result of such thoughts and actions is rebirth as an animal. If you generate an animal mind, an animal mind results, although not necessarily an animal body. As I mentioned, some people have animal-like minds. Either can result: rebirth as an animal or as another kind of being with an animal-like mind.

Q. To survive in Western civilization, we have to earn money. To earn money for food, clothing and the like for ourselves and our family, we have to have a job. In other words, we have to voluntarily put ourselves into some form of suffering. Please could you offer some thoughts on that?

Lama. Yes, I understand that in the West, to preserve your life you have to work and make money. Now, most people work for somebody else. Therefore, instead of simply craving for money, instead of thinking only about the money, sincerely offer your services to your boss; offer your life to that other sentient being. Whether you work for the government or some private company, you're still working for some other sentient being. So instead of thinking, "I want money, therefore I work," instead of having that logic in your mind, think that you are working for others; dedicate your work to others.

Also, we need to preserve our precious human body to use it intelligently for inner growth. Our body is sort of on loan, like a rented house. We have to look after it so that we can practice Dharma properly. Therefore attachment isn't the only reason to work; we can work with pure motivation and the highly respectable aim of benefiting society and other sentient beings. Therefore, if you are wise, working for money is not necessarily negative.

The most important thing is to dedicate whatever you do to others. That is of prime importance. Not emotionally—"Oh, I'm on Lama's Tibetan Buddhist trip"—but by recognizing that attachment is the root of every problem that you have ever experienced, from the time you were born up till now. Mahayana Buddhism stresses the importance of the pure thought of *bodhicitta* above all else and complains bitterly about how attachment is the worst problem of all, but there's a vast amount of psychological explanation behind these statements. I can't explain it all to you in just five days. Nevertheless, you have to know that Mahayana Buddhism does contain such wonderful teachings on human psychology.

Q. Does Buddhism recognize a higher being than the Buddha?
Lama. No, but that's a good question. There's no higher being than the Buddha but you have to understand what "buddha" means. Buddha

doesn't mean a person in a yellow robe sitting somewhere holding a begging bowl. It means a mind that has reached beyond attachment, beyond the dualistic mind. The nature of such a mind is what we call buddha. Therefore buddha is neither form nor color; it has nothing whatsoever to do with material substantiality. The characteristic nature of buddha is exclusively mental—universal knowledge-wisdom. That is what we call buddha, and when you reach that level you too become buddha; there is no difference in attainment between you, Lord Buddha or any other fully enlightened being.

Q. Do you create negative karma if you do a good action but you're not sure if you're doing it for yourself or others?

Lama. First of all, if you're not sure why you're doing something, better not do it. Be wise. Before you go ahead and do something, check up. For example, if you want to give somebody a piece of fruit, first check your motivation. Is this act of giving simply an ego trip? Will it benefit the other person? Can you give without miserliness? You don't want to find yourself in the situation where you give somebody an apple and a couple of hours later think, "I wish I hadn't given him that apple; now I have nothing to eat." That's not right giving.

Q. What if after you give, you think, "Aren't I good for giving him that apple"? Is that ego? Is that negative?

Lama. If you overemphasize how good you are, that's mistaken, but if you think that it was good that you gave it to him because it helped purify your miserliness, that's OK. That works. You have to know what effect your actions have as well as what your motivation is for doing them.

Q. When you open your head chakra, do you get psychic powers?

Lama. I think I understand what you're asking. If you approach opening your head chakra, raising your kundalini—or whatever other terminology you use—with wisdom and a perfect method, you can transform the negative aspect of your inner nervous system into blissful wisdom. Instead of your nervous system being blocked, you've opened the door to wisdom. But if you are unwise, practicing such techniques can be very dangerous. Mahayana Buddhism does contain methods for activating your kundalini energy but you need to have reached a certain level of spiritual development before you're qualified to practice them. If you try them with a mind possessed by lower, sensual desire, if you practice those techniques with attachment, for sense pleasure, as an ego trip, instead of having a positive effect they can affect you negatively. Therefore, you have to be very careful.

Q. Do people who reincarnate as animals have any choice in the matter?

Lama. They have no choice. If they did, there's no way they'd choose to be reborn as an animal. Remember the two departments I've been talking so much about? The association of ego and attachment are in control. We ourselves have no freedom. Even though we're human beings with this powerful, precious, human body, look at our minds—we have almost no freedom whatsoever. Look back through your entire life, at what has happened to you from the time you were born until now. Have you freely chosen everything that has happened to you or not—where you live, for example? Mostly you've had no choice; it's karma. You think that you chose to come to this meditation course but perhaps there's more to it than that. There's a deeper, karmic reason that you're here. Wherever you go, there's a karmic reason.

Q. Surely it's true that the more you evolve spiritually the less chance there is to be reborn an animal?

Lama. That's very true. The more you progress, the less reason there is to receive an animal rebirth. What happens is that as you develop in a positive direction, your negative imprints get burnt. It's like when you burn seeds, they lose their power to grow. Therefore, even though your past non-virtuous actions have left negative karmic imprints in your mind, when you make spiritual progress, they automatically get burnt and can no longer bring their suffering result. As you continue to evolve, your positive mind develops, you start to get more control over your mind, your wisdom increases and automatically the two departments of ego and attachment decrease. Then there's less space for the animal mind to function and less chance that you'll be reborn in that form.

But as I mentioned before, just because you have been born human this time doesn't mean that you can never again be reborn as an animal. Also, some humans have the mind of an animal; some people have more suffering than birds. Therefore don't think that after receiving this excellent human body it's impossible to go back to such a horrible form.

Q. I disagree that you can be reborn an animal once you have reached the human level.

Lama. Then why are some humans more miserable than animals and why are some people's minds worse than those of animals? Some people may be outwardly human but inwardly worse than animals. What's the difference? You cannot say that human beings are so highly developed that they will never regress. It's the mind. I'm not saying that the body is higher; it's the mind. If they have a human body but the mental functions of an animal, what's the difference?

Q. I'm saying that you don't get to be happy until you've gone through some kind of miserable suffering. Until you learn from your lower situation, you can't advance to a higher one. Since you have to start somewhere in the human kingdom, it's more logical that you're going to start with a suffering human incarnation and then slowly work up to a better, more fully realized one rather than be thrown out of the ranks of humans altogether just because you didn't have enough wisdom to make it.

Lama. How can you prove that? How can you prove that life has to always get better and better? You're assuming that modern scientific evolutionary theory is correct—that lower forms evolve into better and better ones and never regress. But science simply looks at life as physical matter.

Q. I'm not referring to that. I'm saying that you might sometimes waste an incarnation because you didn't learn the lessons you were supposed to, but in that case you remain at the same level. You don't go back.

Lama. Really? You can remain as a ten-year-old child? Impossible. You can't even keep your mind at the same level for an hour. How can you remain the same for years? That's a wrong conception that completely disregards impermanence.

Q. What I'm saying is that you come into this lifetime to learn certain lessons. You have a small amount of free will, but if you choose the wrong path, unwittingly or fully aware, then obviously you have not learnt the lessons you came to learn. Therefore, next time around you have to go through the whole trip again.

Lama. I understand your point but I'm saying that it's impossible for anything physical or mental to stay the same. Everything always changes. You can't remain on the same level. Nor is it true that you always have to progress. It's possible for the mind to degenerate.

Q. Can a human who is reborn as an animal learn something from that experience so that it doesn't have to be repeated? Can you realize at the time that it's a bad state of existence?

Lama. It's possible that as a person is passing into rebirth as an animal there'll be an instant of recognition of what's happening, but that moment passes immediately and the person then has to live out the karma of having an animal mind. Before a karmic result ripens there's always the possibility of changing it completely but once it has ripened there's nothing you can do. You are stuck in that particular bodily form until the karma to experience it has finished.

Note, by the way, that some animals' possessing certain abilities— for example, vultures can telepathically perceive dead meat at great distances—doesn't mean that they are intelligent. Such karmically-determined abilities aren't wisdom.

Q. When bodhisattvas reincarnate for the purpose of enlightening other sentient beings can they choose the form they take?

Lama. Yes, higher bodhisattvas have complete freedom to choose. They check up to see what's most beneficial—East or West, male or female and so forth—and take rebirth in an appropriate body. Their only purpose is to benefit others; there's no thought of their own welfare.

Q. How do you deal with negative energy that arises in the mind during meditation?

Lama. If the negative energy is purely mental it will disappear simply by your recognizing it, as I described before. If there's a physical component, like pain, you can try to transform it into bliss. You can also try the breathing exercise.

Breathe in deeply as I described before, push your diaphragm down, pull your inner pelvic muscles up, compress the two energies just below the level of your navel and concentrate at that point—you'll automatically feel a blissful, physical sensation. When that happens, concentrate on that feeling as strongly as you can and automatically your negative energy will be transmuted into understanding wisdom. That's a good way to get rid of negative energy and ignorance but there are many other methods as well.

Q. How do you avoid falling asleep during meditation?

Lama. First you have to know the process by which sluggishness arises so that you can recognize it from the start. Sleepiness in meditation doesn't come openly; it sneaks up on you. If you're aware you can observe your mind begin to go from light to dark. A foggy darkness begins to descend; then it gradually gets darker and darker, your gross sense perception slowly disappears and finally you're asleep. That's how sleep comes; not all of a sudden. We think we fall asleep straight away because we're unconscious. If you check up wisely you will see that it happens gradually.

We call the early part of that process sluggishness—a small impression of darkness. As soon as you notice it starting you should apply the antidote, which is to clarify and brighten your object of concentration. If you do this the fogginess will disappear and you won't fall asleep. At the first sign of sluggishness, visualize light. In meditation, strong, clear light prevents you from falling asleep just as it does when you're in bed at night.

Q. If you are reborn in a pure land do you have to reincarnate back on Earth?

Lama. It's up to you. If you're selfish, you can stay there; if you care about others you'll come back down to the human realm.

Q. Can one be reborn in a pure land with a selfish mind?

Lama. Yes, it's possible. There are many degrees of selfish mind. We actually classify them into nine different levels—the gross, intermediate and small levels of selfish mind, each of which is divided into great, medium and small. As you begin to purify selfishness, you start with the great gross level, then the medium gross level and so on down to the small level of the small. But it takes time to purify the selfish mind all the way down to its most subtle level.

The problem is that when we're happy we tend to forget other sentient beings' suffering. Take, for example, the *arhat*. Someone who is incredibly concerned with his own ego problems practices meditation until he reaches perfect, single-pointed concentration. He then focuses on the ultimate nature of his own mind until he realizes emptiness and discovers the everlasting blissful peace of liberation, or nirvana. He has worked for this experience so hard for so long that once he attains it he forgets other sentient beings and just wants to stay there forever, enjoying his concentration on everlasting bliss. It's no doubt a great achievement but selfish from the Mahayana point of view.

The meditation course

Thank you so much for your interesting questions but now we have to stop. Five days is a very short time to understand this subject. It takes time. If you ask the more experienced students, they'll tell you that even our usual one-month meditation course is nothing.[5] At those courses we have teachings, books, discussion groups, debate and much meditation, but it's still a very short time.

Therefore, at this course I'm more interested in having you gain some meditational experience by putting a few techniques into action than I am in giving you a huge amount of factual information. If I were to try to teach you too much intellectual philosophy you'd freak out. I'd rather you come away thinking, "Yes, this meditation course really helped me. Something in my mind has changed." Of course, intellectual information is necessary but five days is too short for me to impart much.

Therefore just put your mind into action as much as you possibly can. Don't expect to receive realizations; just act. If you do, perhaps even in

[5] Here Lama is referring to the annual meditation course taught each fall at Kopan Monastery, Kathmandu, Nepal, by Lama Zopa Rinpoche.

this short period you'll experience the sweet taste of the honey of Dharma wisdom. That experience can help solve all your psychological problems. It's possible. If you just get intellectual information, there's no action, no experience, no change in your mind and no interest in the subject. Anyway, if intellectual information is all you want you can study Buddhism at university. You can ask, "What is karma, dear professor?" I tell you, if you compare what a college professor tells you about karma with what we are doing here, you'll see a big difference. But don't just believe me; check it out for yourself. Ours is a very different kind of school.

My approach is to expose your ego so that you can see it for what it is. Therefore, I try to provoke your ego. There's nothing diplomatic about this tactic. We've been diplomatic for countless lives, always trying to avoid confrontation, never meeting our problems face to face. That's not my style. I like to meet problems head on and that's what I want you to do, too. The experience of an atom of honey on your tongue is much more powerful than years of listening to explanations of how sweet it is. No matter how much I tell you about the wonderful sweetness of honey, you're still going to be thinking, "Well, maybe it is, maybe it isn't."

Anyway, if you dedicate the five days of this meditation course to other sentient beings, with nothing for yourself, that takes care of everything. That kind of motivation is most worthwhile.

I've seen many young Westerners who've been into all kinds of trips. They love to talk about their experiences: "I went to a meditation course. This Tibetan lama taught some amazing stuff...." But even though you did that course, nothing in your basic nature changed. You got nothing out of it to make you happy. Taking Dharma teachings as just another trip is a waste of time.

However—forget about realizing enlightenment—if the teachings you take help you see things more clearly, make your life easier, improve your communication with others and make you friendlier toward other sentient beings, taking them has been most worthwhile. You have gotten more out of them than simply dry, intellectual knowledge.

And when your ego does arise, when you suffer, when difficult minds plague you, instead of feeling as if a nail had been driven into your body, think, "I'm not the only one that has to go through this. Even now, countless other sentient beings are experiencing the same kind of thing."

Look at yourself right now. Look at your own agitated, uncontrolled mind. When you begin to perceive your own nature you start to have compassion for yourself. When you start to have compassion for yourself you start to have genuine compassion for others. Compassion for others starts with yourself; the realization of true compassion comes from you. First understand your own situation, then you'll feel kinship with and compassion for the countless other living beings. Otherwise your compassion is mixed with attachment. Love and compassion for others come from understanding their nature and situation.

Normally we say, "I love you, I love you." Check up if that's really love. Perhaps you should be saying, "I'm attached to you, I'm attached to you." Love and attachment are completely different in nature.

Therefore, when problems arise, instead of getting overly concerned, "I have a problem with this meditation course; I have a problem," instead of getting too emotional, "I have a problem," instead of focusing too much on "I," when a problem arises, observe closely how your ego interprets it and don't just blindly follow that interpretation. Wait. Check up.

Even when you get back home, keep checking. Don't think that checking in this way has nothing to do with concentration. It takes a lot of concentration. If your mind is preoccupied with too many mundane things, this kind of checking does not come easily. It's not like the checking you apply to your business affairs. It requires strong introspection, wisdom and an alert state of mind.

That's all for now. Thank you very much. Thank you.

Every Problem on Earth Comes from Attachment

Y OU ARE MOST FORTUNATE, having this chance to put much effort of body, speech and mind into seeking inner reality, your true nature. If you check back how you have spent most of your life, you will see just how fortunate you are to have the opportunity of making this search even once. Extremely fortunate.

I'm not just making this up—"Oh, you're so good"—trying to make you proud. It's true. However, to really discover that all human problems—physical and mental—come from attachment is not an easy job. It takes much time.

For example, if you're having difficulty at this course you might start thinking about home: your warm house, your comfortable bed, chocolate cake. You remember all these nice things. Then your ego and attachment get to work: "Oh, maybe I should leave. Why should I stay? At least I know I can enjoy myself back home." We all know what's going to happen when you get there, but still, attachment follows your ego's view: "My bed is so good, I'll be so comfortable back home; my family is there, I can relax and do whatever I feel like, I'll be free. Here, I'm not free and I have to try to be serious. Anyway, my serious mind doesn't seem to be functioning, so I might as well leave." Your dualistic attachment kicks in, telling you so much stuff, convincing you until you say, "Yes, yes, yes..." and leave.

So then you get back home and you're sitting in your room and you check up. How silly. Nothing's new. There's no place on Earth where you're guaranteed to find satisfactory enjoyment. Don't think that Tibet must be a fantastic place, a paradise where everything is pleasure. It was never like that. Since dissatisfaction and attachment inevitably come with this body and mind, your samsaric mandala of dissatisfaction accompanies you wherever you go. Even if you flee your own country for a cave in the mountains, attachment will come along. There's no way you can leave it behind.

Trying to face your problems is much more worthwhile than ignoring their root and trying to run away from them. You've been that way before; it's not a new journey, it's the same old trip. You go, you change, you go, you change...on and on like that. In this life alone you've followed attachment on so many trips.

With effort, everything is possible. In order to attain the realization of indestructible, everlasting peace, you have to have an indestructible mind for training. Realizations don't come without your training your mind the right way. First you have to make the determination, "For such a long time I have been servant to the two mental departments of attachment and ego, trying to please them, but in fact, they are my greatest enemy, the root of all my problems, the destroyers of my peace and enjoyment." You have to understand how these two minds occupy and control your internal world.

According to Lord Buddha's teachings, as long as you don't realize that your real enemy is within you, you will never recognize that the mind of attachment is the root of all the problems your body and mind experience. All your worries, depression and everything else come from that. Until you do recognize that, even though you might occasionally have an hour's good concentration, it never lasts. If, however, you see the psychological origin of your problems and understand the nature of attachment and how it works to cause aggression, desire and hatred, your mind becomes very powerful.

When you're in a peaceful environment, you think, "Oh, I'm so peaceful, my meditation is so good, I have such great realizations," but when you're in the street or out shopping in a supermarket and people bump into you, you freak out. Because you're not sitting in meditation but walking around, your mind is completely uncontrolled. However, if you understand the psychology of attachment and how it lies at the root of your various reactions, you will not freak out so easily and will really be able to control your mind, no matter where or with whom you are.

I'm not talking philosophy here but truth based on living experience. In fact, not only Buddhism, but all religions recognize the shortcomings of attachment. Even worldly people talk about its drawbacks. But even though we say the words, "Attachment this, attachment that," we don't really recognize it as the biggest problem on Earth.

Therefore, what I'm saying is, it would be wonderful if you could recognize that your own attachment is the cause of every single problem that you experience. Problems with your husband, wife, children, society, authorities, everybody; having a bad reputation; your friends not liking you; people talking badly about you; your hating your teacher, your lama or your priest—all this truly comes from your own attachment. You check up.

The source of problems

We Westerners always have to blame something external when things go wrong. "I'm not happy; I'd better change this." We're always trying to change the world around us instead of recognizing that it's our own, internal attachment that we have to change.

For example, when you get hurt because somebody calls you greedy, you blame that person for how you feel. Actually, feeling hurt comes from your own attachment. People don't like your attachment-driven behavior so they call you greedy, hurting your ego. Then, instead of accepting their pointing out your selfish behavior, your attachment to always being right, to being perfect, causes you angrily to reject what they say.

The fact that your ego, your wrong-conception mind, cannot accept criticism is itself a big problem. Your ego wants you to be right all the time and your attachment creates its own philosophy of life: "I don't need anybody's advice, especially that of my parents." Thus your mind is closed. Then as soon as your parents start to talk, without even listening to what they have to say, you immediately reject it. You don't even let them finish speaking. As soon as they begin, your ego starts to hurt. This happens because your ego and attachment have already decided to close that door; as soon as your parents try to open it, conflict begins. That's so silly. How can you say ahead of time that whatever your parents or other people have to say is wrong? But your overestimating ego and attachment make you reject their thoughts completely.

If you realize the shortcomings of attachment, no matter who complains about your behavior, you'll listen to what they have to say and won't start arguing the moment they open their mouth. You'll think about their criticism for a week or a month, checking to see if it's valid or not. If, after contemplating in this way, you still think they're wrong, you can go back to them in a very natural, relaxed way, sit down over a cup of tea and talk it over.

You shouldn't act the same day somebody criticizes you—you're too nervous, your ego is too involved, and all your old, ingrained thought patterns are too close to the surface. Therefore don't react immediately. Calm down, think it over and then respond. That sort of approach is much more constructive.

It's the same when a couple has problems. Instead of immediately starting to argue with your partner, make space. You don't necessarily have to change the substance of your conversation, just the atmosphere. Don't react excitedly. Make space for your point of view to grow in the other person's mind. It's important to know this psychological approach.

Attachment makes you think, "He's my father; I'm his child"; "She's my wife; I'm her husband." The moment you start to think like that, you're asking for trouble. Attachment always creates conflict and makes things difficult. Instead of thinking, "I want to help others," you grasp with expectation, "He's my father, therefore he should look after me." All you want to do from the very start is to take advantage of others. As long as your motivation comes from attachment you'll have difficulty communicating.

It's a bit surprising, isn't it? Here at this course you and I are communicating well with each other. Why? You don't know anything about me. You've come to this course, you're sitting there listening to me, but still we communicate. On the other hand, you've known your parents all your life, you've lived with your husband or wife for many years, but your communication is not so good. Why is that? Check up right now. Isn't that silly? It's also simple. You don't even know what I am, so how come we communicate with each other? Don't think it's the power of the lama, the power of Lord Buddha's teaching. It's the power of your own mental attitude. Since fundamentally, your mind has space, communication is natural. If you didn't have that fundamental space, no matter what I said, it would just go over your head.

Love and attachment

As long as we are driven by attachment, which follows the wrong conceptions of our ego, everything we do is very superficial. When we say we love others or try to be religious by generating compassion, making charity and so forth, it's all on the surface. This is an insufficient answer to our problems.

If you check up honestly what you really mean when you say that you love someone, you'll find that your "I love you" actually means "I want to take advantage of you." Of course, you don't say that verbally or even think those words, but if you check deeper within yourself you'll find that selfish expectation lies beneath your expressions of affection. You look at somebody and if you see that you can get something from that person, you say, "I love you." This is very poor-quality love. From the Dharma point of view, it's not even love at all. True love comes from understanding that others' problems derive from the attachment deeply rooted in their mind and is based on a correct realization of the nature of these problems. This profound logic gives you a deep reason, a universal reason, for helping others. Ordinary love is narrow, closed-minded and fickle.

As long as your love is ordinary, your narrow mind will keep singling out one object: "You're the only one for me; my only object of love and compassion." This Earth contains countless atoms but you choose only one: "I love this atom." That's such a silly mind; completely silly. There are countless atoms throughout all of space but tied by attachment your squeezing mind chooses only one. Then, whenever you encounter another atom, you feel insecure. "I really love my atom. I'm not sure about this other one." This is how your mind is. You fixate on one atom and mistrust the rest.

When you look at the atom you've chosen, what you see is just a relative projection painted onto that object by your ego. Your ego projects that this is a good object, something you can trust, and believing this appearance to be true, you choose that object to be yours. Then, when you see other objects, you automatically don't like them just because they're different and fabricate all sorts of reasons for your dislike: "I don't like its color, I don't like this, I don't like that." When you get attached to one thing, you automatically feel hatred for others.

Of course, if I use the word "hatred," you're going to interpret it emotionally, but that's not how I'm using it. One of the factors in your mind is dislike, which causes you to disdain certain objects, to close your mind off from certain things. The basic nature of that mind is classified as hatred.

You have these experiences because your mind is unbalanced, unequal. Your internal world is constantly being thrown out of balance by the two extremes of attachment and hatred. Your attachment makes you choose one particular atom; your hatred makes you feel that the other millions of atoms are against you. Perhaps I should use a more psychological term than "against" here, but I'm not sure what it would be. "Rejection" might be better. Because of attachment, you have the extreme mind of acceptance, and because of hatred, you have the extreme mind of rejection; automatic rejection of other. These extremes of thought make your mind unhealthy.

More shortcomings of attachment

When we function normally as human beings, we communicate well with each other and seem to be quite healthy. However, those two sick minds—the extremes of grasping acceptance and blind rejection—are always with us. When the conditions are suitable they surface and make us clinically ill. I'm not trying to scare you but you have to be aware of what's lurking in your mind, just waiting to come out. Therefore it's most worthwhile to constantly check your mind. If you do, you'll never have any reason to freak out.

Normally what happens is that you just go along, never observing your mind, and when emotions suddenly arise, you freak out. Sometimes you don't even understand what's happening to you. All the schizophrenic mental defilements, personal problems and suffering of all universal living beings derive from attachment.

Sometimes you think, "People don't trust me." Perhaps they don't. But other people's mistrust of you comes from your own attachment. They don't trust you because they sense the bad vibrations of your selfish attachment. If you didn't give off those bad vibrations others would see you as easy to get on with and not be afraid of you.

If you have a neighbor whose gross mind of attachment is strong you're likely to be afraid of him. You avoid going near his house, and if you have to, you do so cautiously, afraid of what he might do. Others avoid him too. This is a common situation; we're all familiar with it. Why does this happen? When people don't like you it's because they can feel the vibrations of your gross emotions of greed and so forth. Even the members of your own family who like each other don't like you. All this comes from your own attachment.

If you are going to learn only one thing from your Dharma studies, it should be that every problem on Earth comes from attachment. If you can realize that, you won't have to worry too much about deficiencies in other areas—"I don't have good concentration." Anyway, concentration alone is not enough. Dividing the entire Buddhadharma into wisdom and method, concentration comes more from the wisdom side of the teachings, while recognizing the faults of attachment and changing your mental attitude come from method.

To discover the everlasting peaceful realization of enlightenment, ultimate inner freedom, you have to practice wisdom and method together. When you do, it's like a powerful elevator whizzing you straight to the top of a tall building. To reach the top of a building quickly, you need both a powerful elevator and electrical energy; to reach the everlastingly peaceful penthouse of your own inner edifice, you need both wisdom and method.

When people talk about evil, they always make it sound as if it comes from outside of themselves. There's no such thing as outer evil. Mahayana Buddhist art might depict horrible-looking demons but this is just symbolic. We never believe that evil is external. Evil is nothing other than the manifestation of ego and attachment. If somebody asks, "What is evil?" the answer is attachment. Attachment is evil; ego is evil. If you want to know the words for evil, they're ego and attachment.

The kindness of others

Every happiness and benefit you have ever experienced has come from others. When you were born, you came from your mother's womb with nothing. You didn't even have any clothes. Your parents gave you clothes, milk, care and attention. Now that you have grown you have clothes and many other things. Where did they come from? They came from the effort of other sentient beings. Maybe you think it's because you have money. You can't wear money. If other people hadn't made the fabric you wouldn't have any clothes. The cake you enjoy is also the result of others' effort. If they hadn't put effort into making the cake you wouldn't have any. It's the same with all your other samsaric enjoyments; everything comes from other sentient beings, from other people's giving it to you.

Is that too hard to believe? Is that too much for you? Think of everything you've done today. The milk you had this morning—it wasn't your own, was it? Similarly, check in detail everything you have. It has all come from others. You were born with nothing. Other people are so kind. Without the kindness of others you'd find it impossible to live.

Don't think that you've come up through society—studying, working, making money—and now you're doing everything yourself. This is just the intellectual way society has developed in order to run more smoothly. Of course, you can't survive without an organized society. Otherwise how would you get milk from the farm and fruit from the orchard to the city or wherever you live? Society has arranged all this to make your life and everybody else's easier. Society is also kind.

Another example of the kindness of others is that of reputation. You're very attached to having a good reputation, of being well liked. How can this happen if you're alone? How do you have a good reputation without other people? Praise—"You're good, you're kind, you're this, you're that"—comes from other people. Reputation, food, clothing—all your enjoyments—come from other sentient beings. Forgetting their kindness and thinking "I did it" is a completely mistaken, totally unrealistic mental attitude.

Check up. All the food in the supermarket comes from other sentient beings' effort. You can't do everything yourself. Other mother sentient beings expended their own energy, brought the food to the supermarket and made it available to you. I'm sure that your ego and attachment have never let you think that other sentient beings are kind. Over the eons that thought has never even crossed your mind. As I'm saying this you're probably thinking, "Oh, that can't be. That's just what Lama thinks." But you really check up. It's important. Truly, I'm not joking.

The practice of Dharma

If you don't check things deeply your spiritual practice is just emotional. You have only a vague notion of what religion is and whatever practice you do is just empty ritual done according to custom. Religion is nobody's custom; Dharma has nothing to do with custom. The practice of religion, the practice of Dharma, is the gaining of understanding realizations. The problem with us is that we are so ordinary that when we look at Dharma, we do so with our senses. Dharma is not a sense object; it has nothing whatsoever to do with sense perception. Dharma is the view of the wisdom mind; it's what wisdom sees.

Seeking the nature of attachment and realizing that all your pleasures and your life itself come from the kindness and effort of other sentient beings do not demand that you be a member of this religion or that. Dharma practice needs no partisanship: "I'm this; I'm that." Just do it; just realize.

Otherwise you hear some artificial idea, pick it up and try to practice it—Buddhism, religion or whatever else you call it—but it all becomes shallow and artificial. You have no understanding; whatever you do is of poor quality, almost hypocritical. Instead of being of benefit and solving your problems, the idea itself just pollutes your mind.

Look, for example, at what the communists tried to do. Their philosophy was that of radical, external change. Trying to change the external world without first changing within is simply asking for trouble. I'm not talking politics here; I'm talking human psychology. Don't have just a superficial view of human problems. You can't change things that way. Look deep, look wide, and don't be content with mere ideas.

You hear some idea and think, "Wow! That sounds good." This is common, especially amongst Westerners. They are so intellectual; they love ideas. They don't care what they are. As soon as they hear something they like, they're out there trying to put it into action: "Oh, what a great idea! I *love* that idea!" But they don't know how to fit action and idea together, which is much more important than simply the good idea itself. If you don't put them together, ideas are like the sky and you're like the earth—the two never meet. Be realistic.

Equalizing others

It's very difficult to equalize things without changing people's mental attitude. You can't force everybody to be equal. It's impossible. Without changing your mental attitude of attachment, it's impossible to equalize everybody. You can, however, completely change your internal world. Without need of radical external change, you can achieve total inner equality and transform your too-extreme mind into a perfectly balanced one. That's the way to equalize others. It is very logical.

When you achieve mental equilibrium beyond the two extremes of attachment and hatred, your inner nature is even and peaceful instead of conflicted. The experience of inner equality also gives you a vision of beauty when you look at the outside world. You can see that beauty lies deeper than the surface, that human beauty lies within the person, beyond the form your sense perception apprehends. This extremely realistic view gives you a warm feeling for others.

How can you exist without relating to other human beings? It's impossible. You can't live without relating to others. Throughout your entire life, your mind and brain relate to others. Therefore, other people have a great influence over what comes into your mind. That's why most human problems come from other human beings. We imitate each other. Human problems don't come from some place far away. To stop them, your attitude and behavior have to become humane.

When you realize how kind other mother sentient beings have been, instead of seeing them as repulsive or undesirable you'll see them as beautiful. Instead of rejecting them you'll have space in your mind to feel true love—profound, deep love for all sentient beings—and this feeling will be based on deep reasons, not superficial ones. You'll feel inner equilibrium instead of the usual extremes of attachment and hatred.

The logical reason for feeling that all sentient beings are equal is that equally, all sentient beings seek happiness, and not one, yourself included, wants to be unhappy. Think, "All sentient beings want to be happy and no sentient being, myself included, wants to suffer. Whenever I experience an unpleasant feeling I want it to stop immediately. Although basically, all sentient beings equally desire happiness and freedom from suffering, out of the countless billions of beings, my fickle mind selects just one to make happy and forgets the others. When I encounter somebody who agitates me I see him as an enemy and want to give him harm, and when an enemy finds good fortune, I get jealous." Such a mind is unrealistic, unbalanced and extreme.

It's as if two equally hungry and thirsty people come to your door. You look at them both but choose only one, "You can come in," and tell the other, "You can't come in. Go away." You know that they're in exactly the same predicament, that they're both extremely hungry and thirsty, but your extreme, narrow mind picks one—"Come in, I love you. Put on some nice, clean clothes; have something to eat and drink"—and completely rejects the other.

This is the action of a narrow, silly, extreme mind. It all comes from the misconception of attachment, an unbalanced mind acting in an unrealistic manner that certainly has nothing to do with Buddhism or any other religion. Even if you check from the scientific, materialistic point of view, it's unrealistic; even ordinary, non-religious people would easily see that this kind of mind is ridiculous.

So what am I talking about here when I tell you to generate a feeling of equality with all living beings in your mind and concentrate on it? Well, the way to do the Mahayana equilibrium meditation is to first do *analytical* meditation—intellectualizing a little on the equality of all sentient beings, as I mentioned above—and then, when you reach the point where at least intellectually you see their equality, let your mind *remain* in that feeling. Enjoy it. It's a remarkable experience. And you should also *maintain* that feeling of equilibrium in your meditation session breaks—walking, eating, whatever you are doing.[6]

It's very important to recognize that all desire, hatred and other delusions and the problems they bring come from attachment and ego. Actually, of the two, attachment and ego, it's ego that comes first. Delusion starts with ego; attachment follows. How is this? The concept of ego builds a projection of "I" and paints that polluted projection with a veneer of qualities. Then, when the I—superficial, artificial and illusory—starts looking at the pleasures of the sense world, it labels certain objects as desirable. From this, attachment arises, sticking, or clinging, to these attractive objects. This, very briefly, is the evolution of attachment.

The moment your ego says "I," you automatically identify yourself as totally separate from other atoms, other people. On the basis of this view of two different things—self and other—you automatically see "I" as the most important one. Then, with attachment, your narrow mind chooses one particular atom as a source of sense pleasure. This then makes you view all other atoms as either irrelevant or as objects of hatred. That's the way it all starts.

[6] See Appendix, the Mahayana Equilibrium Meditation.

In other words, when you perceive the hallucination of the self-existent, independent I, you immediately accept the existence of other. That
other then appears as totally separate from you. If there were no I, there
would be no appearance of other. But you build up that separateness,
and this is where all the problems of samsara come from. All this is the
work of ego, which is a product of ignorance. Ignorance causes ego.

The wheel of life

Lord Buddha demonstrated this graphically when he created the wheel
of life. You must have seen thangkas of this; they're very common.
There are many details, but at the center there's a pig with a chicken's
tail feathers in its mouth. The chicken's beak holds the tail of a snake,
while the snake is shown biting the tail of the pig. The wheel of life is
not just some item of Tibetan culture. It's a deeply symbolic teaching
and was created by Lord Buddha himself.[7]

Once, some disciples were looking for a gift to send to a neighboring,
non-Buddhist king. Lord Buddha told them how to make a painting of
the wheel of life and suggested they send it to the king simply as a work
of art, without any other explanation. After receiving this gift, the king
kept looking and looking at it, until one day he realized what it represented. The art itself spoke to him. He realized that ego, attachment and
aversion were the worst of all poisons and the cause of all suffering. If
you, too, keep Dharma art in your room, it can have a similarly
beneficial effect on your mind.

[7] See His Holiness the Dalai Lama's The Meaning of Life.

It works the other way as well. Take movies, for example. Sometimes what you see on the screen makes you afraid; sometimes it makes you so sad that you cry. It's not reality; it's an illusion. Nevertheless, without discrimination, the mirror of your mind takes in and reflects whatever garbage appears before it. Things you see can have a strong effect on you. Therefore it's very important that you remain aware of how the people and things around you affect your mind. Check up. Are they stimulating attachment or hatred? If you are psychologically alert you can easily tell, but usually you ignore your internal world. Your ego might be in there making a toilet of your mind but you think it's OK; you don't care. However, if someone were to try to build a lavatory on your property right next to your house, you'd freak out, wouldn't you? It's so silly. You don't know what really makes you happy.

In the wheel of life, then, the pig symbolizes ignorance, the chicken, craving desire, and the snake, hatred. It's a perfect external demonstration of how, starting with ignorance, delusions develop in the mind, and it has nothing whatsoever to do with any Eastern trip, lama trip or other kind of trip. It applies equally to all samsaric beings and is simply a scientific explanation of how our internal world evolves.

Wisdom, love and equilibrium

Now you can see why Lord Buddha always stressed that we should abandon ignorance and develop understanding. He wasn't the slightest bit interested in religious games, ritual or theory. His teachings always stressed actions based on wisdom as the only solution to problems.

Lord Buddha's key discovery was that the pollution of ignorance is the root of all problems, and from ignorance come attachment, craving desire and hatred. Therefore, he always emphasized that only an integrated, understanding mind could overcome mental defilements. You can pretend as much as you like that everything's under control, but if you don't have understanding, you can't stop any problem.

If you conquer your worst enemy—the internal enemy of attachment—you will control all external energy, all other people, but if you try to exercise such control using just the power of your ego, it will be impossible. You think you can control others, but you can't. There's no way to attain inner MUNÉ MUNÉ through the power of ego. Remember Lord Buddha's mantra, OM MUNÉ MUNÉ MAHAMUNAYÉ SOHA? Control, great control, greatest control. To realize inner MUNÉ MUNÉ you have to conquer the inner enemy of attachment. If you can do that, you can control anything.

When Lord Buddha was meditating to reach enlightenment, the maras declared war on him and tried whatever they could to interfere with his meditation. At one stage they attacked him with a hail of arrows. In response, he went into single-pointed concentration on equilibrium and universal love and turned all the arrows into flowers. Nothing the maras threw at Lord Buddha could hurt him; he controlled it all with his inner atomic bomb of universal love. With love, he conquered the whole world.

The well-known Tibetan yogi, Geshe Ben, used to say, "When I was a thief, I went about armed to the teeth with knives, spears and arrows, robbing by day and stealing by night, taking whatever my ego and attachment wanted. At that time, enemies were everywhere and samsaric pleasures hard to find. When I became a monk and changed my life, my enemies disappeared, everybody became my friend and now samsaric pleasures have to fight among themselves to get my attention."

This was his experience. At first his wrong-conception mind and attachment made him think that to have friends he had to be powerful, so he spent all his time fighting and killing others. But the more he fought, the fewer friends and the more enemies he had, and his experiences of pleasure were few and far between. Then he realized that his thinking was all wrong, so he gave up his weapons and found that all his enemies had disappeared, all sentient beings were his friends and he had more samsaric pleasures than he knew what to do with.

Take, for example, the situation where you're confronted by an extremely angry person. If, instead of retaliating, you respond peacefully, with love and understanding, your peaceful energy automatically calms that person down. If you respond to anger by getting nervous yourself, all you do is make the other person more agitated than he already is. It's that simple.

Therefore, the only equipment you need to conquer both external and internal enemies is true love. By external enemies I mean the external objects you *label* as enemy because of the way your internal enemy, the two departments of ego and attachment, interprets them. First you develop equilibrium, then gradually bodhicitta.

Here's another example. Say you have an only son. When he does silly things, you know he's being silly but because you love him so much, it doesn't bother you; you accept whatever he does. If somebody else were to do the things he does, you'd freak out—not because of what the person was doing but because of the way you interpret it. Because you see your son as beautiful, even when he does something bad, you can control your anger; you make an exception.

Similarly, if through equilibrium you come to understand the human condition and human nature at its deepest level, just as your positive view gives you control when your son is naughty, so too will you be able to tolerate the stupid behavior of any living being in the universe; just as you see your own naughty boy as beautiful, it won't bother you when others act silly. Since you understand the basic nature of the mind, you see all beings as beautiful.

Also, you know that when your son is being silly it's because he's under the control of his superficial mind; his attachment is following his ego's narrow point of view. You know that he doesn't really want to be silly but he's pushed into it psychologically by his uncontrolled mind. He has no freedom. You feel only more compassion for him. He's oppressed by his two departments of ego and attachment; completely mashed. When your only son is in this predicament, you don't need to tell yourself, "Oh, I should generate compassion." It comes automatically. Because you understand human nature, compassion comes spontaneously; you don't have to generate it artificially.

To summarize, therefore, it is most worthwhile finally to recognize that your own attachment is your own biggest problem and worst enemy. Your problems do not lie outside of you. As a step towards realizing this, you should actualize the equilibrium meditation.

Equalizing others does not mean radically changing the outside world. It's in the mind. Also, as I said before, it's completely logical that you should feel equal with all living beings. With analytical knowledge-wisdom, approach the feeling of equality. When you reach that point intellectually, let your mind abide in the feeling of equality for as long as you can; maintain single-pointed concentration on equilibrium as long as possible. When you get distracted, return to your logical reasoning and again explain to yourself the nature and shortcomings of attachment. When you come to the conclusion that you are equal with others, again let your mind rest in that feeling of equilibrium. Be satisfied with that. Just stay there. That's much better than intellectualizing at that time.

Therefore, in the next session, practice the equilibrium meditation, and I'll see you again after that. Thank you so much.

Vajrapani Institute, 1983

··· 7 ···

Developing Equilibrium

WHEN YOU GET your first taste of equilibrium, even if it's a small one, it's an extremely powerful experience. With that small experience, your realizations have begun; you have started to realize the peaceful mind. Realizations come slowly. They start slowly, develop gradually, and finally become eternal, or everlasting. You probably think that the results of analytical meditation are a long way off: "If I do a five-day meditation course, maybe next year I'll get some peace of mind." Don't think like that; it's a misconception. If you put wisdom into action you'll experience the effects right now; the results will be immediate.

Perhaps you think, "Oh, how can that happen? This is Buddhism; what about karma? If I start creating karma now, surely I'll have to wait for the results. Cause precedes result. How can I meditate for five days and experience the result the next day; meditate for an hour and get the result immediately? That's impossible." If that's how you think, you're wrong. The karma Buddhism talks about is moment to moment reaction, a minute by minute phenomenon. It doesn't necessarily take hours or more to bring a result.

You know how a watch runs. Second by second, an energy force is exerted and the watch reacts immediately. It's the same with the results of meditation practice. You can experience them right away. The effect is right there.

Of course, if you gain an actual experience of equilibrium, nobody else can tell. Realizations can't be seen from the outside. They're not sense objects. But if they were to appear in material form, they would be enormous.

You can see for yourself, even during this short, five-day course, that meditation has an immediate effect. It is very powerful. And you can figure out what will happen if you continue to meditate: "If I keep acting correctly with right understanding and right effort, there's no question that I'll be able to attain everlasting, peaceful realizations and experience eternal joy. When I first heard that kind of talk I was full of doubt. I couldn't believe there was such a state. But now, through my own small actions and with my minimal understanding of the psychological nature of the mind, even though I haven't yet attained any lasting realizations, I can see that if I put my mind in the right direction, I will eventually gain those deep experiences."

This is perfectly true and completely logical. Why shouldn't you be able to develop enlightened realizations? There's not the slightest doubt that you can develop yourself to perfection.

If I were just to hassle you, "Yes, you should have love, you should have love. Yes, you should have compassion, you should have compassion," if I were to keep at you all day, "You should have this, you should have that, you should, you should, you should...," you'd think I was crazy. But there's a method. It's here, right now. All you have to do is use it. It's such a simple thing.

Feeling equilibrium with all living beings without discrimination is not something that you just make up. You're not trying to equalize something that's inherently unequal. What you're trying to do is to *realize* as equal that which is *already* equal. You're trying to overcome the distortion of inequality projected by your two departments that causes you to experience the two extremes of craving desire and intense dislike.

Just look around. Who among us doesn't want happiness and enjoyment? We all do. And who among us wants to suffer? None of us does. In both wanting happiness and wanting to be free of suffering and attachment, we're all equal. Thus we can see how unbalanced our minds are in being so extreme and how much conflict we experience as a result. If we see this clearly, we'll scarcely believe how ridiculous we've been.

Recognizing the actual enemy

You know how angry you get if you're looking forward to a good time and your friend stands you up. You feel cheated: "That's it. I never want to see him again." But he's only cheated you once. The two departments of ego and attachment have been cheating you longer than you can imagine—days, nights, weeks, months, years; all your life; countless lives—and you still want to be friends with them. That's like locking your house with a thief inside.

You must recognize that your real enemy, the thief who steals your happiness, is the inner thief, the one inside your mind—the one you have cherished since beginningless time. Therefore, make the strong determination to throw him out and never let him back in. But be careful how you approach this analysis. Don't feel emotional or guilty; simply recognize your situation with wisdom.

If somebody was to beat you up every day and you never did anything about it your friends would think you were crazy. "Are you stupid? Why don't you hit back," they'd ask. But that's what we're like. Our two departments, especially attachment, beat us up day and night, month after month, year after year, and we completely ignore them. If we check deeply, we'll feel really silly. It's so true, however, that running after your ego's illusory projections and following attachment is really, really silly; much sillier than running after yet another man or woman. That's nothing.

The biggest cheater is inside, not out. Isn't there an expression, "Nobody cheats you but yourself"? It's not a Dharma teaching but nevertheless, it's very true. However, if you interpret it psychologically, it's actually quite tasty. You see? If you have wisdom, even common expressions can have a strong impact on you. Normally you interpret such sayings very superficially and don't give them much thought, but when you begin to investigate your internal world, even things that ordinary people say can have deep meaning. Whatever you hear can become a teaching. Instead of bringing you down, even negative experiences can produce wisdom. Why? Because you understand where everything comes from and why it arises.

You probably think things are pretty good in your country and when I come along and say that this is wrong and that is wrong, you feel, "What's this silly lama talking about? We don't have any problems. He must be talking about his own problems. Don't bring the problems of India and Nepal over here." You're definitely going to think something like that. But if you're honest, when I explain what problems really are and how they arise, you won't be able to contradict me. Of course, anybody can argue anything. In Tibet, we have an expression: "The son who kills his father always has a reason." He can give you a reason for why he killed his father but that doesn't make it right.

The samsaric gods of the formless realm have no gross suffering. Their situation is completely different from ours. They have no gross body, only mind, and their enjoyments are purely mental. They don't have problems like getting a job, going to work, shopping at the supermarket, cooking food and so forth. Therefore it's impossible to teach them Dharma; they have no comprehension of suffering and agitation. While they're in that state, they can't be helped. Similarly, some people in the West think that their lives are perfect and feel extremely proud that they have everything. But it's not true; they don't have perfect enjoyments. They have no real control over their conditions and no true freedom.

Therefore you should decide once and for all to stop bowing down before attachment. "Although I think I'm very intelligent, I recognize now that I have always blindly followed attachment to objects as seen by my ego. I'm not intelligent; I'm silly. I'll never again be ruled by attachment or bow to that destructive mind." It's as if somebody was threatening to kill you with a knife and you were prostrating to that person in gratitude. Just as that would be silly, so is being nice to your attachment.

Do you understand? When you experience the feeling of equilibrium you experience an incredibly universal spaciousness. Your tight, narrow mind becomes completely open because it has come in from the extremes of thought to the middle way. Your mind feels very comfortable and, for the first time, you become truly mentally healthy. This is not just some theory; it's living experience.

Attachment to ideas

Otherwise we know how we are, don't we? We're full of prejudices: "I'm this; I'm that. This religion is good; that religion is bad." We grasp at and cling to our ideas, which only causes us a great deal of conflict. This is so unrealistic. Attachment to ideas only causes problems. Even so-called practitioners of religion fight each other because they're clinging to ideas. This is completely silly and has nothing whatsoever to do with truth, peace, love or religion itself. Religious conflict is based solely upon misconception.

However, we're all guilty of this. For example, after this course, you'll go home and your friend will ask, "Where have you been for the last five days?"

"I went to a meditation course."

"You did what?"

"There was this Tibetan lama. I did a course with him."

"Are you nuts? You're a Westerner; he's from the Himalayas. You don't think you can do a mountain trip, do you? Anyway, Buddhism is silly. We have plenty of everything here in the West; I bet he told you to renounce. I hope you don't believe what he told you."

This is what your friends will tell you and you'll be hurt inside; your ego will be bruised. You're going to think, "I thought I'd had a good time at that course but now my friend's putting me down for having done it." Depending on the situation, you might feel anger, guilt or some other negative emotion, which means there's something wrong with you. If, instead, you can stay relaxed and watch your mind when you're being criticized, that's wonderful and much more realistic.

Anyway, don't be attached to any ideas, even those of Buddhism or whatever else you're doing. Just put your Dharma into action; practice as much as you can. If you can do that, it will be wonderful. If somebody tells you they're following another religion and you feel negative or insecure, that's a mistake. Instead, be glad that that person is seeking inner truth and can see the possibility of developing his or her mind. Instead of feeling jealous or insecure, respect that person and rejoice. If you hurt inside or feel insecure because somebody's following a religion different from yours it means that there's something wrong with your practice, that you haven't recognized the true source of problems and are caught up with ideas of good and bad. Beware of that.

If you practice properly, the result is peace in your mind. Then when somebody says, "That practice is no good," it doesn't affect you. They're only words; how can they change the truth? It's impossible. Words are nothing. But if you're all caught up in your narrow mind, clinging with attachment to ideas and reputation, empty words become huge; for you, an atom of empty words fills the universe. They hurt you badly. All such experiences actually come from your own mind. The words "good" and "bad" cannot change reality.

True love wants others to be happy

When you try to help your parents, friends or anybody else, it might look like you're helping but if you're acting out of attachment in a partisan way you'll see, if you check more deeply, that instead of helping you might actually be giving harm. You've probably tried to help others many times over the course of your life but how often have you actually helped? How often have you made things worse? How many times has your so-called help produced attachment in another person's mind? Check up on that.

When you choose to help others out of attachment it often results in their generating attachment to you. This can only disturb their minds and cause them conflict. It's as if you'd sent a thief to steal their peace of mind. This kind of thief is much worse than the kind who simply steals your furniture. Losing a bit of furniture doesn't hurt too much, does it? Today you have no furniture; tomorrow you can buy some more. Peace of mind is much harder to replace than a few chairs. You can't buy peace of mind in a store no matter how rich you are. Therefore, check up whether your assistance really helps or not. Does it solve problems or create more? That's what you have to determine.

You can see for yourself that the way attachment works is silly. Say we're in a room and a friend comes in with a delicious cake and gives it to only one person, who then sits there eating it without sharing it with the rest of us. We're going to freak out, aren't we? We're going to be completely jealous. That's how our minds are. Instead of rejoicing— "Isn't he kind? He brought a delicious cake all this way for her. I really hope she enjoys it"—we feel hurt and jealous that we missed out. That's how ridiculous our mind is. Check the psychology here. On the surface it looks as if our reaction is all about the cake but if we go into it more deeply we'll find that our minds are really thinking, "What I want is for me to be happy. I don't want her to be happy."

This is not an intellectual thing. Don't object to what I'm saying: "That's not what I think." I know you don't think consciously that you don't want her to be happy, but if you ask the attachment deeply rooted in your mind what it wants, it's going to answer, "I want to be happy. I want the whole cake. I don't want her to have a single piece." If you check deeply, that will be the conclusion you'll come to, even though superficially, you're thinking, "What are you talking about, Lama? I've never thought that." I'm sure you're thinking, "Lama's really raving on. He's bringing his Eastern hungry ghost mind here to the West, where we have plenty of everything. He doesn't know about supermarkets; we have plenty of cake."

Anyway, attachment is attachment. In India, people crave dal, curry and rice; in the West, cake. What's the difference? The craving is the same; it's just the object that varies. Remember what I said before? Attachment doesn't depend so much on the price of something as on the value placed on it by the mind, by attachment. Attachment is really such a silly mind.

Everybody has parents. We all come from parents and we all have problems with them. If there are two sisters and the parents give a present to one but not the other, the ego of the sister who missed out gets hurt: "Why didn't I get a present? They're discriminating." If she were a good friend, if she really loved her sister, she'd feel sincerely, "I'm so happy they gave my sister a present. I want my sister to be happy." But there's no sincerity. Attachment is so sensitive. Something small happens and you freak out. That's all attachment; that's the attachment trip.

Understanding attachment

Perhaps you think I'm talking about attachment too much but you have to know the attachment trip in and out—its nature and how it functions. Understanding attachment is much more worthwhile than all your grasping with attachment at the pleasure of sense objects and far more valuable than all the education you've ever had, which has only taught you how to develop more attachment. If you make yourself clean-clear familiar with the attitude of attachment, the attachment trip and how the mind of attachment interprets things, you'll gain much pleasure. It will make your life much easier and better. You won't need to exert yourself strenuously to develop loving kindness and compassion; it's sufficient just to search for and investigate the way in which all faults come from attachment. Right action, loving kindness and compassion will automatically ensue.

When you recognize the energy force of attachment, pure thought follows automatically. You don't have to strain yourself: "I want pure thought! I must have pure thought!" You don't have to cling to having pure thought. Just understand the motivation of attachment; pure thought will come of its own accord. When pure thoughts come, your life naturally becomes positive. You don't have to generate conscious thoughts of "I should be good; I must be good." You don't need to intellectualize.

As long as you direct your energy into the channel of peace and wisdom it will spontaneously flow that way. You don't need to think too much. Just act in the right way and do your best to gain realizations; that's enough. We always evaluate actions by their appearance: "He did this; that's bad. She did that; that's good." We think that actions are fixed as good or bad. There's no such thing as an action that's always good or bad; actions can't be categorized in that way. It all depends on the mind.

For example, if you do things that are normally considered religious with attachment, they're negative. Outside observers will think that you're doing something good but they'll be wrong. The actual way to judge whether an action is good or bad is by the motivation behind it, not the action itself. You can't predetermine, "This action is always good; that one is always bad." It's up to the motivation. If you are motivated by concern for others and not self-attachment, the action becomes pure, or positive. If you are motivated by attachment, it becomes impure, or negative.

Compassion overcomes attachment

A story from the previous lives of Lord Buddha, the *Jataka Tales*, illustrates this point. In one of his lives as a bodhisattva he was leading a celibate life, meditating in an isolated place, when he encountered a young woman who was so distraught with uncontrolled physical desire that she was suicidal. He felt such genuine compassion for her that he abandoned his celibate life, married her and stayed with her for twelve years. Lord Buddha himself said that this was a wonderful experience; it very powerfully helped destroy his ego and moved him to a plane of higher realizations. Observing his actions judgmentally we'd say that his taking up with the girl was a negative, samsaric action. But actions aren't negative in and of themselves; it depends on the mind. Since he acted out of compassion, it was positive. Lord Buddha himself said that spiritually, giving up his cherished life as a monk in order to save that woman helped him a lot.

We always think "I want" instead of thinking what others want and then acting to help them. That's why all our actions are mistaken. If you are motivated by pure thoughts, even though to ordinary people, whose minds are fixed, your actions might look negative, they are in fact totally positive. You can never tell from the outside. You can only tell if you can see whether they're done with a positive or a negative mind.

Actualizing the purest thought of benefiting all mother sentient beings, Lord Buddha attained perfect enlightenment. Therefore you should think, "I can do the same thing. There's no doubt that this is my path to enlightenment. I, too, should actualize this pure thought as much as I possibly can." Why can't you? It's very simple; there's no obstacle. Don't think that by trying to follow this path you'll be making trouble for yourself. Why should there be trouble? "It's not part of my culture." That's not true. It has nothing to do with what we normally think of as culture. What is culture? Attachment? Projections of ego? If anything is culture, perhaps they are. Otherwise, what is culture?

Trying to release attachment and being concerned for the welfare of other sentient beings are not at all Tibetan culture; they are no particular people's culture. What ordinary people consider culture is that which has been developed by attachment to sense pleasure, and this has nothing whatsoever to do with Dharma knowledge-wisdom. Dharma knowledge-wisdom is nobody's culture. It is only wisdom culture; universal wisdom culture.

Exchanging self and others

Concern for the welfare of all other sentient beings is based on equalizing self and others but, remember, equalizing others does not mean trying to radically alter their external circumstances. That's a wrong conception. You make others equal in your mind and on the basis of equilibrium, practice exchange of self and others.[8]

For countless lives, you have built up attachment based on a polluted hallucination of the object "I," which you have made important above all else. Recognize that this is a false conception that has resulted in mistaken actions. Instead of being attached to your own welfare, transfer that attachment to the welfare of others. Put their happiness first and your ego's happiness last.

Before going to sleep tonight, sit on your bed and do a short meditation on exchanging yourself and others. Switch your attachment from your conception of "I" to others. If you can develop this kind of wisdom, instead of being completely overwhelmed and mashed by any problems that arise, you'll be awakened. Problems will cause you to generate wisdom and will give you added strength and energy to follow the path to enlightenment. Also, the practice of exchanging self and others helps you eliminate fear. All fear and insecurity comes from attachment. Whenever you feel fear, ask yourself where it comes from. Now you have the answer. It comes from too much concern for self, the hallucination projected by the concept of ego.

That's enough for now but you can see how, starting with the breathing exercise, the meditations we've been doing over the course of these past few days support rather than oppose each other.

Today you took the eight Mahayana precepts[9] so tonight you get no dinner. Actually, it's not you who doesn't get dinner; it's your mind of

[8] See Geshe Jampa Tegchok's *The Kindness of Others* for a teaching on this practice.
[9] See Lama Zopa Rinpoche's *The Direct and Unmistaken Method*.

attachment that misses out. This reminds me of a story from old Tibet. When monks were served food in the monasteries, they'd sit in long straight lines and the servers would pass up and down the line doling out the food. They'd start with the senior monks and gradually move on down to the junior ones. On one occasion some delicious yogurt had been offered to the monastery and Geshe Ben, who I mentioned earlier, was there, sitting down the line a bit. As the yogurt was being sloshed loudly into the bowls of the monks up ahead of him he was sitting there worrying, "They're giving those monks too much. There won't be any left for me." Suddenly he became aware of what was going on in his mind so he meditated on how powerful attachment is and how it creates fantasies that have nothing to do with reality. Then he turned his bowl upside down. When the server reached his place, Geshe Ben said, "No thanks; I've already had mine." In this way he punished his selfish ego and attachment for obsessing over the food that was being served. This is a good example of how to practice an antidote to attachment. It's certainly relevant for us.

Anyway, I can guarantee that skipping the occasional dinner will not make you weak or sick, but just to make sure, tonight I'm going to give you a special psychic energy pill. It's made of natural earth and other special substances and in Tibetan is called *chu-len*, which means "taking the essence." So, without too much expectation of getting some psychic energy, instead of an evening meal just take this pill with your tea.[10]

Thank you very much. Thank you and good night.

---

[10] See Lama Yeshe's "Taking the Essence" on the Lama Yeshe Wisdom Archive Web site.

···8···
Taking Suffering and Giving Happiness

W E ARE MOST FORTUNATE to have been able to pinpoint attachment as the greatest of all problems. When we speak of evil, demons and so forth, it's the inner devil of attachment we're talking about. Even though for countless lives we've looked outside ourselves for the source of our problems, there's nothing external to blame. Therefore we should rejoice that we have finally identified this inner cause of all suffering.

We can be quite foolish. Say you're in a spooky old house somewhere with a couple of friends. It's late at night and you're watching horror movies on TV. One of your friends says, "Don't go into the basement; there's something evil down there." Then, if you do have to go down to the basement, you feel scared: "There really is something evil down here." You're so easily prone to superstition. This is completely silly. There's no such thing as external evil and fear of it is simply a projection of the evil in your own mind. If you speculate enough your superstitious mind is sure to produce something and where once you were unafraid you now feel fear. All such foolishness comes from attachment.

Therefore finally recognizing that all these negative things—demons, enemies, evil or whatever other terms are used in everyday conversation, science or religion—come from the inner demon of attachment and bravely changing attachment to oneself into concern for others is both wonderful and wise.

There are countless living beings on Earth but very few know about exchanging self and others. This practice may be very difficult but it's extremely worthwhile. If you can do it, it will help solve all your problems. Changing your outlook in this way transforms whatever misery you perceive into the peaceful path of liberation.

We desperately need a method such as this. Life is suffering; our minds are weak. Exchanging self and others is truly revolutionary and this inner revolution, which has nothing to do with radical external change, completely turns our mental attitude upside down.

If you were to think that Buddhism was simply about sitting in meditation practicing concentration, you might reject it: "My knees hurt; my body wasn't built for this. Buddhism is just a Himalayan lama thing. Anyway, I can't live without working and taking care of my worldly affairs. Dharma is not for me." But Mahayana Buddhism is about much more than just sitting in concentration. If you are wise, you can practice twenty-four hours a day.

Whenever any difficulty or problem arises, instead of getting depressed, be brave. Think, "Fantastic. If this problem had not arisen I might have felt I had no problems. This problem is my teacher; all problems are my teacher. They give me knowledge-wisdom and help me recognize more clearly the nature of attachment. This is so wonderful. May all mother sentient beings' problems ripen upon me right now and may they receive all my merit, fortune and wisdom."

If you have difficulty taking the suffering of others onto yourself, first practice on yourself. The next time your knees hurt when you're sitting in meditation, take that pain onto your ego and let it freak out. Let your ego freak out more and more. Practice that for a week.

Then practice taking onto yourself all the suffering you have ever experienced in your life. Your ego and attachment won't like that either, but let them freak out again. Then slowly, slowly extend your practice to take upon yourself the sufferings of your parents, your friends, all the people in your country and all the people on Earth until you are receiving the problems and suffering of all sentient beings throughout the universe. Then, without hesitation, send out to them all your possessions, happiness and merit.

What is the technique for actually practicing this taking and giving meditation, which Tibetans call tong-len? You combine it with meditation on the breath in what is basically a nine-round breathing meditation.

Start by breathing out through your right nostril. Visualize the air you exhale in the form of white light, the essence of which is all your positive energy and wisdom. This white light radiates to all sentient beings in the six realms of samsara and beyond. It enters their left nostril, goes into their hearts and generates in them great bliss. Visualize the air they exhale in the form of thick black smoke, the essence of which is all their negativity, confusion and heavy suffering. This dark, polluted energy enters your left nostril and goes down into your heart. Don't leave it outside of you; bring it right down into your heart so that your ego and attachment completely freak out.

The nature of attachment is such that when problems arise, it blindly pushes them away. This practice trains your mind to handle negativity, feel compassion for the others and take their suffering and problems onto yourself, which in turn helps you overcome self-cherishing and cherish others more than yourself.

Do the above cycle of breathing white light out through your right nostril and black smoke in through your left three times. Then breathe out through your left nostril and in through your right three times. Then breathe out and in through both nostrils together three times. At the end of each nine rounds concentrate for as long as you can that you and all other sentient beings have been completely purified of all suffering, negativity and dualistic mind and are fully enlightened, experiencing everlasting bliss that pervades your entire body and mind. When you lose focus on this, repeat the nine rounds once more. Repeat this cycle again and again for the duration of the session.

Don't think that this is just a fantasy and that doing this meditation makes no difference to the suffering of yourself and others. Actually, it is a profound practice and each time you do it, it brings you and all other sentient beings closer to enlightenment. The greatest obstacle to enlightenment is self-cherishing, and taking on all the suffering, karma and delusions of all sentient beings and giving them all your happiness and merit is best way of overcoming it. The most effective way of training your mind to overcome self-cherishing is to practice tong-len meditation.

Conclusion

Now we have reached the end of this short, dream-like course. At the beginning I said that whether or not these five days become beneficial was up to you. To ensure that they did, you therefore dedicated them to discovering the true nature of your own mind for the benefit of living beings throughout the extent of space. But whether or not you benefit from this course probably depends more upon what you do with what you've learned from now on.

During our brief time together you've learned how to do both analytical and placement meditation and it would be wonderful if you could continue to practice these when you get home. Of course, as the old Tibetan saying goes, "Meditation without study is like armless rock-climbing." In other words, you have to have something to meditate on when you do analytical meditation. For this purpose, we strongly recommend the study and practice of the *lam-rim* teachings—explanations of the steps of the path to enlightenment.

You have also learned some other meditation techniques: the vase-breathing meditation, with attention to the feelings throughout your body; dealing with distractions; listening to your inner sound while chanting the mantra of Lord Buddha; recalling your life's experiences, going back all the way to when you were in your mother's womb; the equilibrium meditation; and exchange of self and others with the taking and giving meditation of tong-len.

You also know how to take the eight Mahayana precepts. It would be fantastic if you could do this regularly throughout your life. It is a powerful method of dealing with attachment.

In my talks, the main thing I have tried to do is to give you an experience of how the two departments of ego and attachment are the source of every problem and suffering you and everybody else has ever had. These two minds are your worst enemy and if you are ever to find true freedom and joy, you must get rid of them forever.

Therefore dedicate your life to developing the wisdom understanding the nature of your own mind and working for the happiness of others. Try your best to avoid harming others and generate a warm feeling for all sentient beings.

Thank you so much for coming to this course. I myself have had a wonderful experience. Thank you; thank you so much.

··· Appendix ···

The Mahayana Equilibrium Meditation

This meditation was practiced at the Dromana course. Meditate in the first person and pause for contemplation between paragraphs.

Think: It is never enough to gain only self-liberation. Attachment to personal peace and striving solely for this is both selfish and cruel.

Visualize that you are surrounded by all sentient beings, with your mother seated to your left and your father to your right. In front of you, visualize an enemy; someone who dislikes you or wishes you harm. Behind you, place your dearest friend; the person to whom you are most attached. To the side, visualize a stranger; someone for whom your feelings are neutral.

Think: There is no reason at all for me to be attached to and help my friend or to hate and harm my enemy.

If I were to strive for only my own self-peace, there would be no reason for me to have been born human. Even as an animal, I could strive for this. The various animals have the same aim as many highly educated people—self-happiness—and also create many negative actions, such as fighting with and destroying enemies, cheating others with political mind and so forth, all in the pursuit of their own happiness. There is almost no difference between them except their shape.

The main purpose of my having been born human is to strive for and achieve higher aims—to bring every sentient being to everlasting happiness. This is something no animal can ever do.

Just as I wish to avoid suffering and find happiness, so, too, do all other sentient beings. Therefore, I and all other sentient beings are equal, and there is no logical reason for me to care more about myself than others or to harm enemies or any other sentient being.

For countless rebirths I have been discriminating other beings as friend, enemy or stranger with the self-I consciousness. Chandrakirti said, "Where there is self-I consciousness, there is discrimination of other." From discriminated partisanship between self and other, attachment and hatred arise.

All misfortune arises from acting under the influence of these negative minds.

The self-I consciousness causes attachment to self, which produces attachment to my own happiness.

The entire range of negative minds arises from the above.

Anger is caused by greed and attachment and makes me discriminate against whoever disturbs my happiness, producing the enemy.

Attachment creates the friend, who helps, and determines the enemy, who hinders.

Ignorance labels those who neither help nor hinder as strangers.

Anger makes me hate and harm the enemy; attachment makes me cling to and help the friend; and ignorance makes me see the stranger as having a permanent self-nature. By acting under the influence of these negative minds, I lead myself into difficult and suffering situations.

Attachment creates danger and suffering for myself and others. The whole Earth is in danger of exploding. Attachment offers no peace and brings only suffering.

Since beginningless time, the two negative actions of helping out of attachment and harming out of anger have thrown me into samsaric suffering, making it impossible for me to achieve the perfect peace of liberation and enlightenment.

Negative actions leave negative imprints on the consciousness; these ripen into endless experiences of suffering. If I continue to behave in this way, I will experience the same suffering over and over again for eons and will never receive any realizations or enlightenment itself.

The three objects of friend, enemy and stranger are false and have been labeled incorrectly for extremely temporal reasons. The current friend, enemy and stranger have not always been friend, enemy and stranger in my countless, previous lives. Even the enemy of last year can this year become my friend and yesterday's friend become my enemy today. It can all change within an hour and does so because of attachment to food, clothing and reputation.

A scripture says, "If you try for a moment to befriend an enemy, he will become your friend. The opposite occurs if you treat a friend like an enemy. Therefore, the wise, understanding the impermanent nature of temporal relationships, are never attached to food, clothing or reputation."

Lord Buddha said, "In another life, the father becomes the son; the mother, the wife; the enemy, a friend. It always changes. In cyclic existence, nothing is certain."

Therefore, there is no reason to be attached to friends or to hate enemies.

If the ignorant, self-I conception and its objects were true, the three designations of friend, enemy and stranger should have existed from countless previous lives and should continue to exist through the present to beyond enlightenment. This makes complete nonsense of the concept of enlightenment, since the Buddha's sublime, enlightened mind is completely free of the delusions and imprints that create such distinctions.

Out of his compassion, Lord Buddha taught the equilibrium meditation so that I, too, might become free of delusions, imprints and ignorant discrimination. The concepts of friend, enemy and stranger are false because they and their basis are totally illusory. There is no self-I.

My problems are created not by the enemy but by me. In my previous lives, I harmed others through ignorance and the results of this return in this life, causing me hardship and suffering.

Lord Buddha said, "In previous lives, I have killed all of you before and you have all slaughtered me. Why should we now be attached to each other?"

Chandrakirti said, "It is foolish and ignorant to retaliate to an enemy's attack with spite in hopes of ending it, as the retaliation itself only brings more suffering."

Therefore, there is no reason to retaliate.

The enemy is the object of my practice of patience, which helps me overcome my anger. I should not hate this enemy, who brings peace into my mind.

The enemy is infinitely more precious than any material possession. He is the source of all my past, present and future happiness. I should never hate the enemy. Any possession can be given up for his peace.

An enemy is my greatest need, the source of all beings' enlightenment, including my own. The enemy is my most precious possession. For his peace I can give up myself.

From now on I must never hate or harm the enemy or any other being.

The enemy harming me mentally and physically is under the control of his negative mind. He is like the stick that someone uses to beat another. There is no reason to get angry or to retaliate by harming the enemy. It is not his fault; just as the pain I experience from a beating is not the fault of the stick.

If I had clear wisdom I would see that harming others out of hatred is harming myself out of hatred. Obviously, I should not harm others.

All sentient beings, including the enemy, are the object of Lord Buddha's compassion. The numberless buddhas hold the enemy and all other beings dear to their heart. Therefore, harming another, even slightly, is like harming the infinite buddhas.

The Buddha always considers all sentient beings, including enemies, to be more important than himself. Mindlessly harming another being for my own benefit is the act of a mind of stone.

The enemy and all other sentient beings have been my mother countless times. The holy body, speech and mind of the infinite buddhas are servant to all beings, enemies included. Therefore, I must never give harm to any other being.

Not harming my worst enemy—the ignorance in my mind—and destroying an outer enemy instead is like killing a friend by mistaking him for an enemy. I should not harm the outer enemy but the inner one, the actual cause of all my suffering.

    Because of transcendent realizations based on the equilibrium meditation, no bodhisattva would ever see another sentient being as an enemy, even if they all rose against him or her.

The enemy is merely a concept created by my hatred, just as friends and strangers are concepts created by my attachment and ignorance. I should not believe the distorted perceptions of my negative minds.

If I investigate with my wisdom eye, I will never find my attachment's friend or my hatred's enemy anywhere, neither inside nor outside their bodies. Wisdom tells me that these are merely names.

For all these reasons, I can now clearly see how foolish and nonsensical I have been over beginningless lifetimes.

If you can realize this equilibrium meditation it will become your most priceless possession. Equilibrium brings peace to numberless beings and all your future lives.

Colophon

This meditation comes from Lama Zopa Rinpoche's meditation manual, The Wish-fulfilling Golden Sun of the Mahayana Thought Training. Rinpoche has described it as more than the standard equilibrium meditation as he has added a number of techniques for overcoming anger and developing patience.

··· Bibliography ···

Gyatso, Tenzin, His Holiness the Dalai Lama. *The Meaning of Life: Buddhist Perspectives on Cause and Effect*. Translated and edited by Jeffrey Hopkins. Boston: Wisdom Publications, 1992.

———. *Practicing Wisdom*. Translated and edited by Geshe Thupten Jinpa. Boston: Wisdom Publications, 2005.

Tegchok, Geshe Jampa. *The Kindness of Others: A Commentary on the Seven-Point Mind Training*. Boston: Lama Yeshe Wisdom Archive, 2006.

Yeshe, Lama Thubten. *Becoming Vajrasattva: The Tantric Path of Purification*. Boston: Wisdom Publications, 2004.

———. *Becoming Your Own Therapist & Make Your Mind an Ocean* (combined edition). Boston: Lama Yeshe Wisdom Archive, 2003.

———. *The Bliss of Inner Fire: Heart Practice of the Six Yogas of Naropa*. Boston: Wisdom Publications, 1998.

———. *The Peaceful Stillness of the Silent Mind*. Boston: Lama Yeshe Wisdom Archive, 2004.

Zopa Rinpoche, Lama Thubten. *The Direct and Unmistaken Method of Purifying and Protecting Yourself: The Practice and Benefits of the Eight Mahayana Precepts*. Boston: Lama Yeshe Wisdom Archive 2002.

———. *The Wish-Fulfilling Golden Sun of the Mahayana Thought Training: Directing in the Short-cut Path to Enlightenment*. Kathmandu: Kopan Monastery, 1974. It may be found at www.LamaYeshe.com.

··· Glossary[11] ···

(Skt = Sanskrit; Tib = Tibetan;.)

anger. A coarse mind that sees its object as repugnant and whose function is destructive; one of the six principal delusions.

arhat *(Skt).* Literally, foe destroyer. A person who has destroyed his or her inner enemy, the delusions, and attained liberation from cyclic existence.

attachment. A deluded mind that sees its object as attractive and sinks into and cannot separate from it; one of the six principal delusions.

bodhicitta *(Skt).* The altruistic determination to reach enlightenment for the sole purpose of enlightening all sentient beings.

bodhisattva *(Skt).* Someone whose spiritual practice is directed towards the achievement of enlightenment. One who possesses the compassionate motivation of bodhicitta.

buddha *(Skt).* A fully enlightened being. One who has removed all obscurations veiling the mind and has developed all good qualities to perfection. The first of the Three Jewels of Refuge. See also *enlightenment, Shakyamuni Buddha.*

Buddhadharma *(Skt).* The teachings of the Buddha. See also *Dharma.*

Buddhist. One who has taken refuge in the Three Jewels of Refuge—Buddha, Dharma and Sangha—and who accepts the philosophical world view of the "four seals": that all conditioned things are impermanent, all conditioned things are dissatisfactory in nature, all phenomena are empty and nirvana is true peace.

chakra *(Skt).* A center of psychic energy; there are several throughout the central axis of the body, for example, in the perineal area and at the navel, heart, throat and crown of the head.

---

[11] A more extensive glossary may be found at www.LamaYeshe.com.

Chandrakirti (*Skt*). The sixth century AD Indian Buddhist philosopher who wrote commentaries on Nagarjuna's philosophy. His best known work is *A Guide to the Middle Way* (*Madhyamakavatara*).

chu-len (*Tib*). Literally, "taking the essence." A special pill prepared from various sacred and other substances according to tradition. Tibetan meditators would use them for sustenance in remote areas when food was scarce. Lama Yeshe used to make his own, which he sometimes distributed to his students.

compassion (*Skt: karuna*). The sincere wish that others to be separated from their mental and physical suffering and the feeling that their freedom from suffering is more important than one's own. A prerequisite for the development of bodhicitta.

consciousness. See *mind.*

cyclic existence (*Skt: samsara; Tib: khor-wa*). The six realms of conditioned existence, three lower—hell, hungry ghost (*Skt: preta*) and animal—and three upper—human, demigod (*Skt: asura*) and god (*Skt: sura*). It is the beginningless, recurring cycle of death and rebirth under the control of delusion and karma and fraught with suffering. It also refers to the contaminated aggregates of a sentient being.

delusion (*Skt: klesha*). An obscuration covering the essentially pure nature of mind, being thereby responsible for suffering and dissatisfaction. There are six principal and twenty secondary delusions; the main delusion is ignorance, out of which grow desirous attachment, hatred, jealousy and all the others.

Dharma (*Skt*). Spiritual teachings, particularly those of Shakyamuni Buddha. Literally, that which holds one back from suffering. The second of the Three Jewels of Refuge.

dualistic view. The ignorant view characteristic of the unenlightened mind in which all things are falsely conceived to have concrete self-existence. To such a view, the appearance of an object is mixed with the false image of its being independent or self-existent, thereby leading to further dualistic views concerning subject and object, self and other, this and that and so forth.

ego. The wrong conception that "I am self-existent"; the self-existent I. The view of the self held by a mind that has not realized emptiness.

emptiness (*Skt: shunyata*). The absence of all false ideas about how things exist; specifically, the lack of the apparent independent, self-existence of phenomena.

enlightenment (*Skt: bodhi*). Full awakening; buddhahood. The ultimate goal of Buddhist practice, attained when all limitations have been removed from the mind and one's positive potential has been completely and perfectly realized. It is a state characterized by infinite compassion, wisdom and skill.

equilibrium. Absence of the usual discrimination of sentient beings into friend, enemy and stranger, deriving from the realization that all sentient beings are equal in wanting happiness and not wanting suffering and that since beginning-less time, all beings have been all things to each other. An impartial mind that serves as the basis for the development of great love, great compassion and bodhicitta.

four noble truths. The topic of the Buddha's first teaching. The truth of suffering, the cause of suffering, the cessation of suffering and the path to cessation of suffering as seen by an *arya*, or noble one—one who has direct realization of emptiness.

Gelug (*Tib*). The Virtuous Order. The order of Tibetan Buddhism founded by Lama Tsong Khapa and his disciples in the early fifteenth century.

Great Vehicle. See *Mahayana.*

Hinayana (*Skt*). Literally, Small, or Lesser, Vehicle. It is one of the two general divisions of Buddhism. Hinayana practitioners' motivation for following the Dharma path is principally their intense wish for personal liberation from conditioned existence, or samsara. Two types of Hinayana practitioner are identified: hearers and solitary realizers. Cf. *Mahayana.*

ignorance (*Skt: avidya; Tib: ma-rig-pa*). Literally, "not seeing" that which exists, or the way in which things exist. There are basically two kinds, ignorance of karma and ignorance of ultimate truth. The fundamental delusion from which all others spring. The first of the twelve links of dependent arising.

inherent existence. What phenomena are empty of; the object of negation, or refutation. To ignorance, phenomena appear to exist independently, in and of themselves, inherently. Cf. *emptiness.*

Kagyu (*Tib*). The order of Tibetan Buddhism founded in the eleventh century by Marpa, Milarepa, Gampopa and their followers.

karma (*Skt; Tib: lä*). Action; the working of cause and effect, whereby positive actions produce happiness and negative actions produce suffering.

lama (*Tib; Skt: guru*). A spiritual guide or teacher. One who shows a disciple the path to liberation and enlightenment. Literally, heavy—heavy with knowledge of Dharma.

lam-rim (*Tib*). The graduated path. A presentation of Shakyamuni Buddha's teachings in a form suitable for the step-by-step training of a disciple. The lam-rim was first formulated by the great India teacher Atisha (Dipamkara Shrijnana, 982-1055) when he came to Tibet in 1042. See also *three principal paths*.

Lesser Vehicle. See *Hinayana*.

liberation (*Skt: nirvana; Tib: thar-pa*).The state of complete liberation from samsara; the goal of a practitioner seeking his or her own freedom from suffering (see also *Hinayana*). "Lower nirvana" is used to refer to this state of self-liberation, while "higher nirvana" refers to the supreme attainment of the full enlightenment of buddhahood (see also *Mahayana*).

Lord Buddha. See *Shakyamuni Buddha*.

love. The sincere wish that others be happy and the feeling that their happiness is more important than one's own; opposite in nature from attachment.

Mahayana (*Skt*). Literally, Great Vehicle. It is one of the two general divisions of Buddhism. Mahayana practitioners' motivation for following the Dharma path is principally their intense wish that all mother sentient beings be liberated from conditioned existence, or samsara, and attain the full enlightenment of buddhahood. The Mahayana has two divisions, Paramitayana (Sutrayana) and Vajrayana (Tantrayana, Mantrayana). Cf. *Hinayana*.

mantra (*Skt*). Literally, mind protection. Mantras are Sanskrit syllables usually recited in conjunction with the practice of a particular meditational deity that embody the qualities of that deity.

meditation. Familiarization of the mind with appropriate objects. Technically, there are two types of meditation: analytical and placement, or stabilizing.

merit. Positive imprints left on the mind by virtuous, or Dharma, actions. The principal cause of happiness.

Milarepa. A great Tibetan yogi (1052-1135); one of the founders of the Kagyu school of Tibetan Buddhism. Famed for his exemplary relationship with his teacher, Marpa, his amazing asceticism and his songs of realization, Milarepa is one of the legendary figures in the history of Tibet.

mind (*Skt: citta; Tib: sem*). Synonymous with consciousness (*Skt: vijnana; Tib: nam-she*) and sentience (*Skt: manas; Tib: yi*). Defined as that which is "clear and know-ing"; a formless entity that has the ability to perceive objects. Mind is divided into six primary consciousnesses and fifty-one mental factors.

mind training (*Tib: lo-jong*). A genre of teaching that explains how to transform the mind from self-cherishing to cherishing others, eventually leading to the development of bodhicitta (see also *tong-len*).

Nagarjuna (*Skt*). The second century AD Indian Buddhist philosopher who pro-pounded the Madhyamaka philosophy of emptiness.

nihilist. In the context of this book, someone who, upon hearing or reading about emptiness, comes to the mistaken conclusion that nothing exists; for example, that there's no cause and effect of actions or no past and future lives. An extreme view, like its opposite, eternalism.

nirvana (*Skt*). See *liberation*.

Nyingma (*Tib*). The "ancient" order of Tibetan Buddhism, which traces its teach-ings back to the time of Padmasambhava, the eighth century Indian tantric mas-ter invited to Tibet by King Trisong Detsen to clear away hindrances to the establishment of Buddhism in Tibet.

paramita (*Skt*). See *six perfections*.

Paramitayana (*Skt*). The Perfection Vehicle; the first of the two Mahayana paths. This is the gradual path to enlightenment traversed by bodhisattvas practicing the six perfections through the ten bodhisattva levels (bhumi) over countless eons of rebirth in samsara for the benefit of all sentient beings. Also called the Sutrayana. See also *Vajrayana*.

Prajnaparamita (*Skt*). The perfection of wisdom.

pride. A deluded mind that holds an inflated or superior image of oneself, pre-venting spiritual attainment and causing one to disrespect and look down upon others; one of the six principal delusions. Seven types of pride are described.

prostration. In Buddhism, the practice of bowing down in respect before one's teacher, a holy object or an altar; there are many different ways of making prostrations.

purification. The eradication from the mind of negative imprints left by past non-virtuous actions, which would otherwise ripen into suffering. The most effective methods of purification employ the four opponent powers of reliance, regret, resolution and the application of antidotes.

refuge. The door to the Dharma path. A Buddhist takes refuge in the Three Jewels fearing the sufferings of samsara and having faith that Buddha, Dharma and Sangha have the power to lead him or her out of suffering to happiness, liberation or enlightenment.

reincarnation. Rebirth, generally within cyclic existence; one body dies and according to karma, the consciousness goes on to the next life, via the *bardo*, or intermediate state, body.

Rinpoche (Tib). Literally, "precious one." Generally, a title given to a lama who has intentionally taken rebirth in a human body to continue helping others.

samsara (Skt). See *cyclic existence.*

Sangha (Skt). Spiritual community; the third of the Three Jewels of Refuge. Absolute Sangha are those who have directly realized emptiness; relative Sangha are ordained monks and nuns.

sentient being (Tib: sem-chen). Any unenlightened being; any being whose mind is not completely free from gross and subtle ignorance.

Shakyamuni Buddha (563-483 BC). Fourth of the one thousand founding buddhas of this present world age. Born Siddhartha Gotama, a prince of the Shakya clan in north India, he taught the sutra and tantra paths to liberation and enlightenment; founder of what came to be known as Buddhism. (From the *Skt: buddha*—"fully awake.")

six perfections (Skt: paramita). Charity, morality, patience, enthusiastic perseverance, concentration and wisdom. See also *Paramitayana.*

suffering. The state of being trapped in cyclic existence under the control of delusion and karma; the subject of the first of the four noble truths.

sutra (*Skt*). A discourse of Shakyamuni Buddha; the pre-tantric division of Buddhist teachings stressing the cultivation of bodhicitta and the practice of the six perfections. See also *Paramitayana*.

Sutrayana (*Skt*). See *Paramitayana*.

tantra (*Skt*). Literally, thread, or continuity; the texts of the secret mantra teachings of Buddhism. Often used to refer to these teachings themselves. See also *Vajrayana*. Cf. *sutra*.

Tantrayana (*Skt*). See *Vajrayana*.

Theravada (*Skt*). One of the eighteen schools into which the Hinayana split not long after Shakyamuni Buddha's death; the dominant Hinayana school today, prevalent in Thailand, Sri Lanka and Burma, and well represented in the West.

thought transformation. See *mind training*.

three baskets (*Skt: tripitaka*). The three divisions of the Dharma: vinaya, sutra and abhidharma.

Three Jewels. The object of refuge for a Buddhist: Buddha, Dharma and Sangha.

three principal paths. The three main divisions of the lam-rim: renunciation, bodhicitta and right view.

tong-len (*Tib*). Literally, "giving and taking"; the meditation of taking all sentient beings' suffering onto oneself and giving them all one's happiness and merit.

Triple Gem. See *Three Jewels*.

Tsong Khapa, Lama Je (1357-1417). Founder of the Gelug tradition of Tibetan Buddhism and revitalizer of many sutra and tantra lineages and the monastic tradition in Tibet.

tulku. See *rinpoche*.

twelve links of dependent arising. The twelve steps in the evolution of cyclic existence: ignorance, karmic formation, consciousness, name and form, sensory fields, contact, feelings, attachment, grasping, becoming, or existence, birth and aging and death.

Vajrayana (*Skt*). The adamantine vehicle; the second of the two Mahayana paths. It is also called Tantrayana or Mantrayana. This is the quickest vehicle of Buddhism as it allows certain practitioners to attain enlightenment within one single lifetime of this degenerate age. See also *tantra.*

vase-breathing. A meditation on the breath in which one focuses on inhalation, holding and exhalation of the breath. It was taught by Lama Yeshe at the Dromana course.

wheel of life. Usually refers to a pictorial representation of cyclic existence, whose rim is the twelve links of dependent arising and whose hub shows the three poisons of ignorance, attachment and hatred.

wisdom. Different levels of insight into the nature of reality. There are, for example, the three wisdoms of hearing, contemplation and meditation. Ultimately, there is the wisdom realizing emptiness, which frees beings from cyclic existence and eventually brings them to enlightenment.

LAMA YESHE WISDOM ARCHIVE

The LAMA YESHE WISDOM ARCHIVE (LYWA) is the collected works of Lama Thubten Yeshe and Lama Thubten Zopa Rinpoche. The ARCHIVE was founded in 1996 by Lama Zopa Rinpoche, its spiritual director, to make available in various ways the teachings it contains. Publication of books of edited teachings for free distribution is one of the ways.

Lama Yeshe and Lama Zopa Rinpoche began teaching at Kopan Monastery, Nepal, in 1970. Since then, their teachings have been recorded and transcribed. At present we have more than 10,000 hours of digital audio and some 60,000 pages of raw transcript on our computers. Many recordings, mostly teachings by Lama Zopa Rinpoche, remain to be transcribed, and as Rinpoche continues to teach, the number of recordings in the ARCHIVE increases accordingly. Most of our transcripts have been neither checked nor edited.

Here at the LYWA we are making every effort to organize the transcription of that which has not yet been transcribed, edit that which has not yet been edited, and generally do the many other tasks detailed below. In all this, we need your financial help. Please contact us for more information:

LAMA YESHE WISDOM ARCHIVE
PO Box 356, Weston, MA 02493, USA
Telephone (781) 259-4466; Fax (678) 868-4806
info@LamaYeshe.com
www.LamaYeshe.com

The Archive Trust

The work of the LAMA YESHE WISDOM ARCHIVE falls into two categories: archiving and dissemination.

Archiving requires managing the recordings of teachings by Lama Yeshe and Lama Zopa Rinpoche that have already been collected, collecting recordings of teachings given but not yet sent to the ARCHIVE, and collecting recordings of Lama Zopa's on-going teachings, talks, advice and so forth as he travels the world for the benefit of all. Incoming media are then catalogued and stored safely while being kept accessible for further work.

We organize the transcription of audio, add the transcripts to the already existent database of teachings, manage this database, have transcripts checked, and make transcripts available to editors or others doing research on or practicing these teachings.

Other archiving activities include working with video and photographs of the Lamas and digitizing ARCHIVE materials.

Dissemination involves making the Lamas' teachings available through various avenues including books for free distribution, books for sale through Wisdom Publications, lightly edited transcripts, audio CDs, DVDs, articles in *Mandala* and other magazines and on our Web site. Irrespective of the medium we choose, the teachings require a significant amount of work to prepare them for distribution.

This is just a summary of what we do. The ARCHIVE was established with virtually no seed funding and has developed solely through the kindness of many people, some of whom we have mentioned at the front of this book and most of the others on our Web site. We sincerely thank them all.

Our further development similarly depends upon the generosity of those who see the benefit and necessity of this work, and we would be extremely grateful for your help.

The ARCHIVE TRUST has been established to fund the above activities and we hereby appeal to you for your kind support. If you would like to make a contribution to help us with any of the above tasks or to sponsor books for free distribution, please contact us at our Weston address.

The LAMA YESHE WISDOM ARCHIVE is a 501(c)(3) tax-deductible, non-profit corporation dedicated to the welfare of all sentient beings and totally dependent upon your donations for its continued existence.

Thank you so much for your support. You may contribute by mailing a check, bank draft or money order to our Weston address; by making a donation on our secure Web site; by mailing us your credit card number or phoning it in; or by transferring funds directly to our bank—ask us for details.

LAMA YESHE WISDOM ARCHIVE MEMBERSHIP

In order to raise the money we need to employ a fulltime editing team to make available the tens of thousands of pages of unedited transcript mentioned above, we have established a membership plan. Membership costs US$1,000 and its main benefit is that you will be helping make the Lamas' incredible teachings available to a worldwide audience. More direct and tangible benefits to you personally include free Lama Yeshe and Lama Zopa Rinpoche books from the ARCHIVE and Wisdom Publications, a year's subscription to *Mandala*, a year of monthly pujas by the monks and nuns at Kopan Monastery with your personal dedication, and access to an exclusive members-only section of our Web site containing special, unpublished teachings currently unavailable to others. Please see www.LamaYeshe.com for more information.

THE FOUNDATION FOR THE PRESERVATION OF THE MAHAYANA TRADITION

The Foundation for the Preservation of the Mahayana Tradition (FPMT) is an international organization of Buddhist meditation study and retreat centers, both urban and rural, monasteries, publishing houses, healing centers and other related activities founded in 1975 by Lama Thubten Yeshe and Lama Thubten Zopa Rinpoche. At present, there are more than 130 FPMT activities in over thirty countries worldwide.

The FPMT has been established to facilitate the study and practice of Mahayana Buddhism in general and the Tibetan Gelug tradition, founded in the fifteenth century by the great scholar, yogi and saint, Lama Je Tsong Khapa, in particular.

Every two months, the Foundation publishes a wonderful news journal, *Mandala*, from its International Office in the United States of America. To subscribe or view back issues, please go to the *Mandala* Web site, www.mandalamagazine.org, or contact:

FPMT
1632 SE 11th Avenue, Portland OR 97214
Telephone (503) 808-1588; Fax (503) 808-1589
info@fpmt.org • www.fpmt.org

The FPMT Web site also offers teachings by His Holiness the Dalai Lama, Lama Yeshe, Lama Zopa Rinpoche and many other highly respected teachers in the tradition, details about the FPMT's educational programs, audio through FPMT radio, a complete listing of FPMT centers all over the world and in your area, and links to FPMT centers on the Web, where you will find details of their programs, and to other interesting Buddhist and Tibetan home pages.

DISCOVERING BUDDHISM AT HOME
Awakening the limitless potential of your mind,
achieving all peace and happiness

This fourteen-module program is designed as an experiential course in Tibetan Buddhist philosophy and practice. The teachings contained herein are drawn from the Gelug tradition of Lama Tsong Khapa, a great 14th century saint and scholar. These teachings come in an unbroken lineage from Shakyamuni Buddha, who first imparted them some 2,600 years ago, since when they have passed directly from teacher to disciple down to the present day.

The realizations of Shakyamuni Buddha cannot be measured but it is said that the Buddha gained direct insight into the nature of reality, perfected the qualities of wisdom, compassion and power, and then revealed the path to accomplish those same realizations to his disciples. The Buddha's teachings have been presented in various ways by different holy beings over the centuries to make them more accessible to those of us who did not have the opportunity to meet the Buddha himself. Lama Tsong Khapa was one such holy being and his teachings on the *lam-rim* (graduated path to enlightenment) are the heart of the Discovering Buddhism at Home program.

In addition, two contemporary masters, Lama Thubten Yeshe (1935-1984), and Lama Zopa Rinpoche (1945-), have imparted these teachings to their students in a deep and experiential way, leading thousands of seekers to discover for themselves the truth of what the Buddha taught. The methods and teachings found in this program also reflect the unique styles of these two great teachers and are meant to help students get an experiential taste of the Buddha's words.

There are two levels of participation that you may choose from when you embark on this program. Within each of the fourteen modules there are discourses, meditations and other practices, readings and assessment questions. As a casual student you may do some or all of the above as you wish. Alternatively, you can engage in this program as a certificate student, in which case you will see on the summary sheet that comes with each module the requirements to be fulfilled. With each module you also receive a Completion Card, which you have to fill out if you want to get a certificate. Although we recommend doing the modules in order, you don't have to. When you have completed all fourteen cards you can receive the certificate of completion issued by the Education Department of FPMT and FPMT's Spiritual Director, Lama Zopa Rinpoche,